THE LIGHT OF EVENING
A Brief Life of Jack Foley

Jack Foley

THE LIGHT OF EVENING
A Brief Life of Jack Foley

Jack Foley

Academica Press
Washington~London

Library of Congress Cataloging-in-Publication Data

Names: Foley, Jack (author).
Title: The light of evening : a brief life of Jack Foley / Jack Foley
Description: Washington : Academica Press, 2021. | Includes references.
Identifiers: LCCN 2020951921 | ISBN 9781680538892 (hardcover) |
ISBN 9781680538908 (paperback) | ISBN 9781680538915 (ebook)

A much earlier version of this autobiography appeared in Gale Research's Contemporary Authors Autobiography Series in 1996. This version has been corrected and considerably expanded.

For Sean, Kerry, Sangye
and to the memory of my late wife, Adelle

SAN FRANCISCO'S LAWRENCE FERLINGHETTI
"Chaplin is dead, but I'd wear his bowler."
drawing by Jack Foley

CONTENTS

THE LIGHT OF EVENING

I continue my reading of cheap novels. It satisfies
... my taste for imposture, my taste for the
sham, which could very well make me write on my
visiting cards: "Jean Genet, bogus Count of
Tillancourt."

*

I learned only in bits and pieces of that
wonderful blossoming of dark and lovely flowers:
one was revealed to me by a scrap of newspaper;
another was casually alluded to by my lawyer;
another was mentioned, almost sung, by the
prisoners – their song became fantastic and
funereal ...

—Jean Genet, *Our Lady of the Flowers*

What is a life but stories—stories we tell ourselves, stories
we tell others, stories others tell about us? Out of these stories we
fashion—what? I am *writer, husband, father, poet, teacher, friend,*
"radio personality," occasional cook, householder, amateur
guitarist, sometime tap dancer, jobless person, performer, student,
widower since 2016, any number of other things. And now,
biographer. How was "he" as a poet? you may ask. How was "he"
as a lover? Was his cooking all right? Who is "he" when "I" see
"myself" from the objective point of view? Who is doing the seeing?

Where did "he" get his lamentable habit of putting words in quotation marks and italics? What are these words anyway? Will they tell me anything real about "him"?—*Adrift,* to use the title of one of his/my books. But what did "he" mean by that?

A year ago (1994) I was told by my doctor that I had diabetes. The doctor told me to read up on the subject but if I saw any references to "blindness, impotence, and death," not to worry, that wasn't the kind of diabetes I had. Appropriately enough, my earliest memory is of being fed candy. My mother and I are lying on a bed. I believe we are in a hotel room in Port Chester, New York, a city in the southeastern part of the state, on Long Island Sound, population approximately 25,000. We have recently moved to Port Chester from Philadelphia. My father is not there. My mother is, if I'm not mistaken, weeping violently. I am being given candies which were actually named "Chocolate Babies" but which my mother and others regularly referred to offensively as "N— Babies." My mother is making an effort to shut me up. I am probably about three years old and I am "eating babies." My mother perhaps wishes that real babies could disappear as easily as these babies can. If I remember correctly from later experience, the candies are delicious, but at this moment they are not quite doing the job. My mother is trying to prevent me from asking a question which tears her apart. *Where is Daddy? Is Daddy coming back?* She doesn't know, though at some level, I think, she realizes that he *will* come back. She knows but she does not know, and the uncertainty is tearing her apart. The uncertainty is tearing me apart too, and so I keep asking. I am like an awful witness to the failure of her life.

After that, nothing. I don't know how the story turned out. Perhaps my father walked through the door the next moment and reassured everyone. Certainly, we were able at times to maintain the fiction of being a happy family as, here, we were maintaining the fiction of being an unhappy one. Perhaps this is a "screen memory," standing as an emblem for many individual events. When the pressure of circumstances became too much for him, my father would simply *disappear*: later I learned that he would go on "binges." But he would always come back. Perhaps I was reminded of these disappearances when I heard stories of a Christian god who also disappears—disappears for centuries—but who also promises to come back. That god too is frequently represented as a baby, and, under certain circumstances, like the Chocolate Babies, he is "eaten."

*

> The past is a foreign country. They do
> things differently there.
> —L.P. Hartley, *The Go-Between* (1953)

> Today, you can see that the happiest men
> All got rhythm.
> —Ira Gershwin, "Slap That Bass" (1937)

Much of what I'm writing here is ancient history, stories which people who know me now don't know. My pattern, in more ways than one, has been that of the shape-shifter: I am fifty-five years old as I write this in 1995; if you saw a photograph of me at eighteen you would have trouble recognizing me. What you are reading here will be considerably revised in 2020, when I turned eighty.

My father, John Harold Aloysius ("Jack") Foley: 1895-1967. Slightly taller than I, thin, jet-black hair (my hair is brown), with a touch of the dandy. People would say, "He reminds me of Fred Astaire." My mother, Juanita Teriolo (later shortened to Terio): 1898-1964. She hated the name "Juanita" and so called herself "Juana," shortened to "Juan," which she pronounced "Ju-an," with two syllables. Plump, dark, with intense, piercing eyes. He was Irish. She was Southern Italian (Calabrese), with perhaps some Spanish blood. I was their only child: born August 9, 1940 (a Leo), Fitkin Hospital, Neptune, New Jersey, outside of Asbury Park, where my parents were living. A war baby. The *Dick Tracy* comic strip for that day features an attempt to arrest "Yogee Yamma," an exotic-looking man wearing a turban. My father, forty-five years old, was working at Fort Monmouth as a telegrapher. I was christened "John Wayne Foley." Later, the confirmation name "Harold" was added. (My father claimed not to be able to spell his own confirmation name, "Aloysius.") The naming had nothing to do with the popular movie actor, John Wayne. My father wanted to name me after his deceased brother, but the parish priest convinced him that Wayne was no proper saint's name, so I was named John after my father with Wayne as my middle name.

The name was a rare gesture on my father's part towards his family. There were several Foley children. "We were fairmers"—farmers—my father told me. They were living in Elmira, NY. He was, I believe, the youngest, "the baby of the family," his sister said. His brother, Wayne, somehow learned to tap dance. He taught the art to my father and helped him to enter the dazzling world of show business. My father performed in vaudeville as well as in one of the last minstrel companies, presided over by George "Honeyboy" Evans. He appeared primarily in shows produced by his mentor, George M. Cohan, the producer of the "Honeyboy" Evans show. My father's sister Goldie was part of that world too. She was a Ziegfeld Follies girl, a spectacular beauty (my father would say, "a swell-lookin' dame"), and perhaps in some sense the love of my father's life. "We'd go everywhere together," he told me, reminiscing. "Everybody thought we were sweethearts." Pause. *"But we weren't."* He was hardly a sophisticate. He used to tell the story of being in the subway as a young man and seeing a sign saying "Smoking Prohibited." He was with a friend who wanted to smoke. My father told his friend the sign meant "you could go ahead and smoke." (I'm sure he eventually discovered the meaning of the term: he lived through "Prohibition.") He also told me of being with the songwriter, Jimmy McHugh. They were passing the poetry section of a library when McHugh turned to my father and, pointing to the section, said, "Jack, it's all in there." In general my father didn't tell stories about our family. He told stories about his friends in show business. Later I realized that the friends were almost always—perhaps always—Irish. The people he knew in show business became his real family. He married one of them—Laura, one of the dancing Wood Sisters. Evidently, that marriage (about which I knew nothing as a child) was short and disastrous. The lyrics to one of the songs my father wrote go:

> They all love my wife
> They all love my wife
> She makes all of them fall
> When I go to bed she's at a dance
> When I wake up she's in a trance
> Oh, what a home sweet home I've got it!

Or, more poignantly:

> Passing my window faces I see
> Most of them smiling none smile for me
> None know I'm lonely or that I'm alone
> Since you have left me home isn't home
> Why weren't you satisfied

Goldie was the only one of my father's siblings I actually met, and by the time I met her her beauty had gone. There was another sister, May, for whom my father wrote a song, and perhaps others. I don't know what became of them. Both my father and Wayne served in World War I, but Wayne died young as a result of the mustard gas he had inhaled. He called for my father on his deathbed but my father couldn't summon the courage to go to him.

Naming me after Wayne was a late—and no doubt rather guilt-ridden—fraternal gesture.

As my father grew older he grew bitter about women. "Put a man in all that make-up, fix his hair, and he'd be just as attractive as any woman." He was not advocating drag. Women baffled him and, finally, frightened him. He wished at last to keep his distance. Another lyric goes, "I did all I could to make you happy, but still you chose to grow cold and forget. / My pillow's wet every night, praying you'll write, goodness only knows why."

My father left show business when vaudeville, which was his primary bread and butter, gave way to the movies and died. In addition, his great mentor and occasional employer, George M. Cohan, lost interest in musicals and made an ill-fated attempt to establish himself as a "straight" playwright. My father opened a dance studio. He received a telegram from Cohan wishing him luck and tendering "kindest personal regards." The venture failed. He turned to Postal Union—where he had worked as a telegrapher during the summers—and then to Western Union, which eventually made him manager of the Port Chester branch. He claimed that the sound of the telegraph key reminded him of tap dancing. Recently I came upon a clipping, a review of one of his performances. It refers to him as a "great" dancer. Since childhood I have collected recordings of vaudevillians: Cohan, Harry Lauder, Nora Bayes and Jack Norworth, Gallagher and Shean, many others. All these recordings bring me closer to my father, whose performing days

were long past when I knew him. "To Americans," writes John E.
DiMeglio in *Vaudeville USA*,

> the vaudevillian...typified the spirit of liberty. Was he
> not utterly free? He travelled across the expanses of the
> great land, and did as he wished on the stage. In the most
> mobile of all nations, that nation's most mobile citizen,
> the vaudevillian, represented something special.
> Vaudeville entertained the family, the sacred core of
> America's strength. Yet the nation had been founded by
> daring adventurers who challenged the unknown. The
> average American had to remain close to home, but not
> the vaudevillian. He was heroic in this sense, meeting
> the challenges of one town after another, one audience
> after another, his very career at stake each time he
> mounted the stage. The theatergoer could share in all
> this. The destiny of the lone figure on stage was in his
> hands.

I think of my father in his suit, with his black hair slicked
back, or in his underwear playing his nightly game of solitaire.
"Your father," one of his drinking companions told me after his
death, "was a goodtimer."

MY FATHER

Once, in the hospital:
"I got all charged up
and danced up the hill
and fell on the ice—
that's what got me here"

he found it funny
that the very things
in which he delighted most

drink and dance
(he was Irish after all)
laid him low

he was the moving glamorous shadow
that stayed in the spotlight
of my childhood
and moves in me still

as I sing
as I dance

as I sing
as I dance

The story of my mother's life seems to have been the story of the longing to go home. Her home town was Perth Amboy, New Jersey, where she met my father. He must have seemed like an embodiment of all the lights of Broadway. She maintained the hope that I would enter show business, and my father did indeed teach me to tap dance. Like my father, my mother came from a large family. When we visited Perth Amboy on Memorial Day there seemed to be relatives everywhere. Her brother Panny ("strong as a bull") was once a wrestler and now called himself an "automobile beautician." I remember her sister Maggie as immensely fat ("it's her glands") and barely able to walk. I was expected to hug Maggie and kiss her, which I did with little enthusiasm. I don't think the people there liked me very much. I was too bookish, I had little interest in—or capacity for—sports. When I learned to play the guitar my mother would force me to bring it to Perth Amboy. Everyone would ask me to play. At first I would refuse. Finally, I would comply. Everyone was sitting around me in utter silence. You could hear a pin drop. The moment I began to play, everyone started to talk.

My maternal grandparents, whom I never knew, operated a store which featured delicious Italian (particularly Calabrese) cooking, my favorite kind of food for many years. My relatives maintained the tradition of good cooking, but I disliked these trips to see people whom I scarcely knew and who scarcely knew—or wanted to know—me. Yet this was the place for which my mother yearned. Port Chester was quite similar to Perth Amboy. It too boasted a large Italian population. Yet my mother was never really able to make friends there. She would make a friend, there would be an intensity of communication, then there would be a fierce argument and that would be the end of that. There were fierce arguments at home, too, but that relationship went on. My parents made an attempt to make me happy, and at times I was. But I was also lonely, on my own a lot, given to imaginative play. There was a great mirror on my mother's dresser. I would play in front of it, watching myself. We listened to the radio (this was "the golden age") and we went to the movies. If I saw a movie in which I identified with the hero, I became the hero the next day. The "movie" became my image in the mirror. Thirty years later I raised the question, "Is the movie screen a window or a mirror? It appears to be a window, but it turns into a mirror." I'm sure my childhood experience had something to do with that question, though I believe there is also something in the nature of movies which encourages one to think of mirrors. Criticism as secret—or, as Oscar Wilde said, the only civilized form of—autobiography.

I suspect that my mother would have preferred for me to have been a girl. There are stories of her dressing me in girl's clothing—my girl ego was named "Geraldine"—but I remember little of this, and I have no temptation to cross dress at this point. When I was in my twenties, my father remarked, in as manly a voice as he could muster, "Well, I thought you were a little, you know, but I guess you're all right." There's a story here too. When I was in high school a male teacher took an interest in me. Like Deborah Kerr in the popular movie, he was planning to offer me a little more than "tea and sympathy." He taught gym and English literature and was responsible for school plays. He knew of my interest in musicals and once hinted that he was planning to cast me in the lead in *Carousel*, but the production never materialized. I must have led him on unmercifully. He was very popular with "the guys," and as far as I know no one ever suspected him except for one teacher, Angela Kelly, who confided to me, "I went out with him." My mother decided to not believe me when I told her the truth about him. "Oh, you're lyin'." He was Italian and rather handsome, so she must have fantasized about him. It was remarkable how strongly her fantasies guided her.

The teacher invited me to accompany him to an excellent Broadway musical, *The Music Man*. He was very careful to ask my parents. He explained that he *could* take me all the way back to Port Chester, but it was a shorter drive to Mamaroneck, where he lived. I could spend the night with him and he could take me to school the next day. He really gave me every consideration. He said I could sleep on the couch or, if I preferred, "bunk in" with him. I chose to "bunk in." He took me in his arms and kissed me. I still remember his voice as he said, "In a moment our eyes will get used to the light and we'll be able to see each other." I felt nothing, no fear but no sexual excitement either. That was that. My experiment had come to its conclusion. I mumbled something about having a headache and rolled over to go to sleep. The next morning he was understandably a little panicky: "I hope nothing happened that bothered you...." I reassured him, "No, no." It was certainly my fault as much as his. I must have been experimenting, wondering about my sexuality. The fact that I felt nothing freed me a little. It only occurred to me recently that, had it been a different man, the results might have been different. Gay men have often figured in my responses to art: Noël Coward, Jess, Robert Duncan, James Broughton, Neeli Cherkovski. I hate the concept of the shadowy homosexual figure who haunts—and taunts—the good American hero in so many American films: the Penguin vs. Batman, for example. Yet my sexuality is finally not all that different from such heroes'. John Wayne once said, "I guess I've proven that I'm no pantywaist." I don't even know what a pantywaist is. But I suppose my encounter with that teacher was such proof for me. "Don't knock it unless you've tried it," the "gay" villain says to Clint Eastwood in one of his films. "What makes you think I haven't," Eastwood replies. Someone in the audience said "Whoa!" at that remark. I suppose my adventure with the teacher was a way of saying "Whoa" too, of putting the brakes on something. I have no idea what became of the teacher. I hope he found someone better suited to him than I was, though the fact that at least one other teacher knew his secret may have meant that he was eventually found out. I wonder how many other people he may have taken to New York!

Though my high school never put on its production of *Carousel*, Port Chester did afford me two moments of stardom. The first of these involved my father. I have some talent for drawing. Since my father worked for Western Union, he had the addresses of various famous people. At his suggestion, I drew pictures of President Eisenhower and sports announcer Bill Stern. My father then sent the pictures to the people I had drawn, hoping that they would greet me as a young Picasso. I received a letter from Eisenhower's press secretary and another from Stern himself. This was written up in the local paper, *The Daily Item*, as "Local Boy Receives Letter From President." There was a photograph of me with my easel; it was featured the next day in my high school home room. I thought it strange that the reporter who wrote the story interviewed only my father, not me. The story rhapsodized, "Who would be next in a boy's heart to the president—who but a figure from the world of sports?" Who indeed.

I wondered what that reporter would have made of my interest in Bernard Shaw (whose prefaces and plays were actively distancing me from Catholicism) and Noël Coward, whom I had seen with Mary Martin in an amazing television special, *Together With Music*. I had a record album, *Noël and Gertie*, with Coward and Lawrence performing the balcony scene from *Private Lives*. Coward (like Burns and Allen or Lucy and Desi) was demonstrating that the unit was not necessarily the single performer, the "lone vaudevillian," but the "team," the man and the woman together. This team was not quite "the family." It represented something different: the search for that mysterious other for whom one yearned and who arose out of one's deepest feelings of loneliness. Indeed, the team suggested that the other could not only be found but even presented to the world. That the other was also *oneself*, something denied or broken off from one's own psyche, only increased the yearning. Thinking of my poetry presentations—my wife and me reading chorally—James Broughton remarked that he thought I was producing an "androgynous form." "King Amour," a poem I wrote in 1986, attempts to deal with such desire:

> How
> is it possible to speak to you?
> We stand
> in different dimensions if we stand at all-you
> in that darkness on the "other side" (flow into it!) What is it?
> "The bareness of the mind the glitter of certain states"-

Dusk. What I can see of the sky is gray. Colors darkening.
Everything failing.

Hope is inseparable from Delusion (Love)....

The second instance of stardom is when I appeared on *The
Ed Sullivan Show* (then called *Toast of the Town*) as a member of
The Port Chester Senior High School Choir. Sullivan had been
involved with Port Chester Senior High—like me, he had been a
student there—and he decided to do a television show about his life,
so he invited the high school choir to perform. In addition, I believe
he was currently living in Port Chester. People tell me they saw him
at one of the Catholic churches, though I never saw him there. The
Choir sang "Beyond The Blue Horizon" and "You'll Never Walk
Alone." It was, as Sullivan used to say, "a rilly big shew," with Bob
Hope, Pearl Bailey, Smith and Dale (Neil Simon's "Sunshine
Boys"), and others. Everyone looked at least ten years older than
they did on TV. Smith and Dale snapped at each other angrily
backstage and Pearl Bailey behaved like a total prima donna. Bob
Hope came over to talk to us but then got distracted by Ed. I
remember having to stand for a long time under the hot, bright lights.
More recently (1991), my friend Ishmael Reed generously described
me in *Time* magazine as a "literary luminary" of California. When
Ishmael told me what he had done, I was so surprised—
flabbergasted—that the only thing I could think of to say in reply
was, "In 1955 I was on *The Ed Sullivan Show*." Ishmael waited a
beat and said, "You've topped it."

It was part of my mother's weirdness that, though she might take a cup of coffee, she would never eat off anyone else's plates. No one was clean enough for her. Every day she scrubbed away at the house in an effort to keep it clean. Later, when she was ill with cancer, she wrote me telling me how exhausted she was, "and the house is dirty." The "house" was in fact a three-room apartment on the top floor of an apartment house. The apartment house had been someone's mansion once, but now it was divided up into apartments. There was a marvelous front yard where we could play catch or even baseball. I never felt quite middle class in that situation. My middle-class friends had houses. They often had their own rooms. I had space in the apartment but not my own room. Middle-class people seemed to live a marvelous life. My mother's urge to clean meant that the house was always in an uproar as she moved furniture around to get at any piece of dirt that might be hidden from her. The houses I visited seemed calm, orderly, like the houses I saw in situation comedies on television. There seemed to be people living the fifties' version of the American Dream: a house, a television set, reliable plumbing. I just wasn't one of them. Someone said to me recently, "You were a rebel even then." But I wasn't a rebel. I was an *outsider*. From my position I could watch people, but it was difficult for me to participate. I was in this respect very similar to a moviegoer. I don't know at what point I began to believe that everything around me was *fictional*, that people's lives were a constant invention. But from my outsider position that is the way it seemed. It wasn't that their lives weren't real. For them, their lives were very real, and many times in my life people have told me their stories. My position as outsider has made me a good listener. But their lives were at a *distance* from mine. That poor teacher whom I led on—there was an entire drama going on for him. It just wasn't going on for me. Yet I could understand him. I was not "a camera" exactly (in Christopher Isherwood's famous phrase), but I was a kind of sponge, even (in Shelley's words) a "sensitive plant"—a nothing, a null space ready to be filled with someone else's being. "Yah," said my friend Larry Eigner to me, "Negative Capability."

Like other women, my mother had been trained to take care of a baby by practicing on dolls. The result of this was not only that the doll "became" a baby; the baby also "became" a doll. My mother selected my clothes and combed my hair for my entire life through high school. I objected at times, but never very strongly. I knew that when I went away to college everything would change. I understood that I needed to please my mother. She was the person with whom I had most daily contact, and she was formidable. Her anger might erupt at any moment. When I was "bad" she would beat me with a special stick. Once, after I had grown and been away to college, she tried to "spank" me again: I grabbed the stick and broke it in front of her. This infuriated her, but it was the end of the spankings. Perhaps most terrifying was the phrase, "Wait till your father gets home," though I soon learned that my father didn't share her anger at such moments. He would come home weary, having perhaps stopped at a local bar on the way. He had no real interest in "disciplining" me. I also knew from Sunday school that it was a mortal sin to miss Mass on Sunday—and if you died in a state of mortal sin you would burn in hell—but neither my mother nor my father ever went to church. When I asked my mother about this she said, "Oh, I got nothin' to wear." Though I never asked my father about the matter, I noted the contradiction. It was perhaps a factor, one of many, in my becoming—without any real "crisis of faith"— an "ex" Catholic. I wrote this during the terrible coronavirus pandemic:

EASTER 2020: THE MAN WHO DIED

another package of weird
toilet paper delivered—
can we find
dishwashing liquid
anywhere—
which Vietnamese
restaurant is open
today—
eggs are scarce
this Easter
—recollections of Syria
2003:
a lovely Muslim man
told me Muslims didn't believe
Jesus died on the cross,
which was why the tomb
was empty,
he went, perhaps, "underground"
for a time

no bishops no kings
no resurrection no christians
desire
is at the heart of it all
we move in the dark
as blind as the characters
in Saramego's novel
moving in a dark contagion
which is somehow "white"—
what is "blind
faith" if not desire
and what is resurrection
but the desire for life
asserting itself
even in the face of death
Which of us wants to die?
All faith is blind
We believe the flowers
that spring up from underground
promise us life
and that the man on the cross
whose body dies and comes back
says the same
and what if it isn't true
what if it isn't true?

.

—contagion
takes us
anyway

It's interesting that people who are dimly aware that they
have done something wrong will often brag to others about what
they have done, hoping that their friends will greet the incident with
delight and approbation—and so will vindicate them. Once I

overheard my mother doing this. She told friends—in front of me!—
that she often got upset when, as a baby, I began to cry and she
couldn't determine the reason. Her solution would be to hit me!
"There," she would say, "now you have a reason to cry." Her friends
greeted this confession as an amusing eccentricity, with laughter.
Nonetheless, she seemed to feel genuine shame at her position in
life. She would occasionally shoplift things. Once, she was caught
and brought to the police station. My father had to rescue her. He
felt that his position in the town—something he was proud of—was
what got her off. Her embarrassment was tremendous. She was also
superstitious and would "read cards" for people (*"strega"*). I believe
she would charge them for this. In addition, she would buy more
food than was necessary and sell the extra cans to her friends at a
reduced price. It was a way of getting a little more pocket money.
She believed she was fooling my father but I discovered that he was
quite aware of it. She would say to me with prophetic vigor,
"Someday you'll know" and "Someday you'll miss your mother"
and also "I wish you could always be little." Any genital exploration
by me was strictly "shameful." Once when she felt I wasn't being
sufficiently sympathetic to her plight she waited till I was alone in
the apartment and phoned me. Unfortunately for her, I recognized
her voice. Pretending to be someone else, she said, "You know your
mommy? I'm going to *kill* her!" I said, "Mommy, stop doing that,"
and she hung up. The incident was never mentioned. When, in 1964,
she was on her deathbed, groggy with sedatives, she seemed to

believe that she was going to hell. It was horrifying. "I'm going down, down," she muttered. I tried to reassure her, "You're going up, up," but she would have none of it: "Not after what *I've* done." I don't know what terrible guilt was upon her. A few moments before she died, she sat bolt upright in the hospital bed, her eyes tightly closed. She began to whirl her arms in front of her, as if she were warding off some unseen enemy. I ran for the nurse. When we returned, the nurse went in ahead of me. She turned to me and said, "She's gone."

Many, many years after my mother's death, I wrote these poems about our relationship:

MOTHER'S DAY

can I remember the warmth and forgive her the beatings
can I allow for the clear narcissism in her affection
and remember the affection
what had she done except me
I was perhaps her only accomplishment
and look how that ended: in tears and anger
the love she felt came crashing down upon us both
can I forgive myself the anger and egotism of adolescence
can I weep for her as a lonely being
whose life was never satisfactory
and who looked to me perhaps as her redemption
"This is my son," she said to a nurse on her deathbed in the hospital,
"ain't he something." there was a pause and she added quietly,
"Oh, he don't care."

she died with the horrible thought that she was going to
hell.
I tried to argue. she said, "Not after what I've done."
God knows what guilt lay on her soul.
her suffering was perhaps her real redemption.
whatever she did she paid for with pain.
time roared between us. had I been older
I might have understood. she had intelligence
but nothing for it to act upon except
the prejudices of her family and her station. I can see her
in my mind's eye, in the photograph that made Judy Grahn
exclaim,
"Oh, she was beautiful," her strong smile and good teeth
that I have inherited. can I say now, and mean it,
as I did as a child, "I love you, mommy"
and thank you for the good that you did for me
though I could not thank you then. How many times I
kissed her
and held her. how much at this moment I miss her
and regret the horrible misunderstanding
that could never, never be solved.
Good night, mother. May you have slept well
through the long corridor of these painful, happy years.
...

FOR MOTHER'S DAY: AFTER MALLARMÉ'S "LES FLEURS"

Ô Mère qui créas en ton sein juste et fort,
Calices balançant la future fiole,
De grandes fleurs avec la balsamique Mort
Pour le poète las que la vie étiole.

like the flesh of a woman, the rose:
avalanches of gold from the ancient sky

and the eternal snow of stars
on the first day, haloes scintillating—
hyacinth, laurel, whiteness of the lily,
heavenly evenings, what touch led to…
balm of Giliad
O Herodias, O Mother
offering love in the dim past (and anger)
a flower opening, but a hand upon my heart

My mother hoped by her advice, example and bullying to control my life. "Don't get married until you're forty." (I married at 21.) But in fact I knew that my life was in my own hands. This was the message of the books I was reading. The only problem was that my life was also *elsewhere*. In Port Chester I was laying low. I would have to wait until I got away for my life, my true life, to begin.

I perhaps summed the matter up in this recent recollection of a musical I saw way back in the 50s:

FANNY

"And now, Eddy Fisher's Fanny,"
was the sniggering joke
that circulated in my home town
when Fisher made his hit recording.
It must have been 1954 or 1955
so I would have been
about 15
(evidently my *annus mirabilis*)
I saw the show:
the aging Pinza of the magnificent accent and purity of
voice
though a pincher of women,

Walter Slezak, whose father had been an opera singer
("What time's the next swan?")
and oh, Florence Henderson
who for me will never be the Brady Bunch's mother
but the appealing ingénue with the lovely soaring voice.
Who could not love her?
And why is Harold Rome never mentioned
in accounts of great Broadway composers?
They're all dead now.
When Warner Brothers made the film
they used Rome's wonderful music only as background:
none of the songs that thrilled my adolescence.
Here's a boy with no heart to give,
not worth one tear you'll cry—
Fanny, oh, Fanny, goodbye!
This morning, remembering over 60 years later
and muttering the tune, I wept.
What was it?
Who was Marius leaving?
I was Marius
and I understood that the great gesture
the great task of the male members
of the American bourgeoisie
was to leave the family.
It was the great life-changing adventure I was to begin.
Now it is almost at an end.
Here's a boy with no heart to give,
not worth one tear you'll cry—
goodbye to my mother, my father,
to the only world I really knew.
The great trumpet blast of *Look Homeward, Angel*
led me forward
but there was a shadow as well

and it was here, in this musical,
in this fable,
in this parting from love
that seemed absolutely necessary
and yet immeasurably sad.
Not worth one tear you'll cry
Fanny, oh, Fanny,
goodbye.

*

...at a distance life awoke, and there was a rattle of
lean wheels, a slow clangor of shod hoofs. And he
heard the whistle wail along the river.

Yet, as he stood for the last time by the
angels of his father's porch, it seemed as if the
Square already were far and lost; or, I should say, he
was like a man who stands upon a hill above the
town he has left, yet does not say "The town is
near," but turns his eyes upon the distant soaring
ranges.

—Thomas Wolfe, *Look Homeward, Angel*

Bios, the Greek word, means life, particularly human life, as
opposed to *Zoon*, a living being, an animal. But we are *both*
"humans" and "animals." Perhaps I should be writing an
autozoography as well as an autobiography: my history as an
animal. What I am doing here is nothing but telling stories, often
stories I have told friends over the years. *How can one break through
stories into something like the life I lived?*

My father was surprised and delighted when I won
scholarship money to go to college. One of the scholarships, the

major one, came from Western Union. Western Union provided three prizes for children of its employees: first prize was a full scholarship to Cornell University in Ithaca, NY. The other two scholarships were less money, but you could go to any school you wished. I won first prize. "Kid, I didn't think you'd be able to go," my father told me, "I didn't have the money." With a probably misplaced zeal I simply *assumed* I was going to college and that the money would somehow take care of itself. Amazingly, it did.

I had come to Port Chester in 1943. When I left in 1958 I understood myself to be a poet. My essay, "Home/Words," in *Exiles* (1996) deals with the moment in 1955 at which I discovered poetry. Someone—probably a teacher, perhaps Angela Kelley, who was Italian but who had married an Irishman—suggested that I read Thomas Gray's poem, "Elegy Written in a Country Churchyard" (1750). I had no idea why the teacher thought the poem would appeal to me. I thought it very unlikely that I would have much interest in it, but I looked it up in the library and took it home...The poem seemed to me the most beautiful *sound* I had ever heard. [It] affected me so deeply that I wanted it to have come out of me, not out of Thomas Gray, and I immediately sat down and wrote *my own* Gray's "Elegy," in the same stanzaic form and with the same rhyme scheme as the original:

> I see the night—the restless, eager night
> That spreads its shadow softly on the day,
> And whispers to the sun's red, burning light

To vanish like a dream and pass away.

I see the night—the darkened mist of night—
And feel the velvet sorrows mem'ries bring;
September's leaves have fallen, old and bright,
And autumn's winds have blown the dust of spring.

I think of days long past, and gone, and dead,
Of all the ancient, withered hopes I've had,
And wonder where the passing hours have fled—
The ghosts of yesterday—forever sad.

O ghosts, my dreams, once breathing, once alive,
Like flower petals in a hurricane,
Were sundered from their stems, no more to thrive,
No more to feel the gentle touch of rain,

No more to hear my reckless, youthful calls,
But banished into bleak eternity,
To come again to me when darkness falls,
As waves upon the seas of memory.

And now the night, with stars and shining lights
All winking, sprightly, like the woodland fawns,
Is fading fast, for with a thousand nights,
There comes the brilliance of a thousand dawns.

Unlike Gray, I took myself as the subject of my elegy. But its mournful tone—and words like "mem'ries"—was directly traceable to him. I understood the state of mind named in Gray's "Elegy" to be the state of mind of poetry itself; and in reacting so deeply to it, I understood myself to be a poet.

It was by no means a simple state of mind. It had to do with the enormous power of words not merely to reflect but to *create* a "reality," a "mood" which moved me away from the daylight world in which I ordinarily functioned and had identity: "I see the *night*...." In some ways Gray's lines hinted at sexuality—surely an issue for me at that time. His rose "blushes" and, virginal, "wastes its sweetness on the desert air"; he writes of "the dark, unfathomed *caves*." Speaking the words aloud let me experience them *physically*, with my own breath, coming out of my own body. In *this* situation, mind and body seemed not to be at odds: Thought seemed sensuous, sensuality seemed thoughtful. Self and other were joined here too. Thomas Gray was a long-dead poet of the 18th Century. It was *his* mind that was being expressed in his elegy. Yet his poem seemed to be expressing my own inmost thoughts. It was almost as if Gray's passionate words allowed him to be reincarnated in my body.

There was of course a "real" Thomas Gray, a man who actually existed and who did a number of things beside write poetry. The Gray I was experiencing was not that person but Gray the poet, the bard. Aspects of both our lives seemed suddenly to fall away, to be of little consequence. What did it matter who the man Thomas Gray was? What did it matter who I was—born in New Jersey, growing up in New York? My powerful reaction to Gray's words allowed me to recognize not only who *he* was but who I was: I "was" a poet. And to "be" a poet meant to be transformed, to move away from the person who lived at 58 Prospect Street and who was 15 years old and who had a mother named Juan and a father named

Jack. Poetry offered me another identity, that of the poet; and, in so doing, it offered me another "home"—that of words. The life I led "at home"—"in my house"—was one thing; the life of words (the wordworld!) was another.

But a person with two homes can be understood as an exile.

When I arrived at Cornell one of my poems had been published in my high school yearbook ("We shall return no more, no more, our days...."). Three short pieces had been selected for an anthology of high school poetry. Another poem had been published in a series called "Yale Penny Poets." (Later I learned that Larry Eigner had a poem in that series as well.) I momentarily considered majoring in math, which I was good at and had enjoyed in high school. But I knew that my primary interests lay elsewhere, and I became an English major. My minor was French literature.

To my surprise, my freshman roommate, Richie Giustra, was both Catholic and a wrestler (the Church militant!). He was about my size and was trying to be nice. His brother had attended Cornell and so Richie knew the campus a little. He showed me around. But we were both a little nervous. When it came time to go to sleep I had some difficulty. Suddenly I heard a favorite piece, Gershwin's *Rhapsody In Blue*, beautifully played. At first I thought the music was coming from a radio, but in fact it was simply in my head. As I "listened" to it I fell asleep. I have always been grateful to Gershwin for that moment:

there—on the edge
of sleep—
guiding me into it.
("Chorus: Gershwin")

Soon one of my dorm-mates tried to get me together with
another English major, Ed Pechter. Ed and I eventually became good
friends, but at this point we circled around each other warily.
Noticing that it had begun to snow, he smiled and said, quoting
Shelley's "Ode To The West Wind," "If Winter comes...." That
settled the matter. The man was at the very least trivializing a great
poem; at worst he was committing blasphemy. I recited the entire
first stanza of the poem and then, without another word, turned and
left. I thought I was punishing Ed for his loose tongue. Ed thought I
was trying to impress him!

"After years of continence," wrote Ezra Pound, "he hurled
himself into a sea of six women" ("Moeurs Contemporaines"). That
is exactly how I felt after Port Chester, though Cornell's 3 to 1 ratio
of men to women made finding the six women a little difficult. "I'm
not oversexed," I used to say, "I'm just undernourished." In any
case, Cornell offered me the opportunity to reinvent myself, and I
went about doing that. I was a writer, a poet, no longer a "brain"—
some sort of oddity—but an "intellectual," something which (unlike
a "brain") might have a sex life. Here, writing poetry seemed
actually to be an advantage. (I was so out of it in high school that
when someone called me a "fag" I had no idea what they were

saying. When I looked the word up in the dictionary all I could find was "*Slang*. A cigarette." It was some time before I discovered the actual meaning of the word.)

I had brought my Gretsch "Ultra-Modern Twin-Pickup 'Miracle Neck' Electric Spanish Guitar" with me to Cornell, but I wasn't sure whether I'd have much occasion to play it. This changed when I met Lou Cataldo, another outsider. Lou was half Italian and half Puerto Rican and called himself a "Ginnyspik." He called me a "Ginnymick." He had been raised in Greenwich Village (of which he spoke with great authority), could play the saxophone and double on bongo drums. He constantly used the word "crazy." We decided that the best way to meet women was to have a band. ("Crazy!" said Cataldo.) We put up advertisements for a "girl singer" in the women's dormitories and held auditions. We got a lot of names, addresses and phone numbers and—a girl singer. When I told this story to someone recently she asked, "Which of you had the affair with her?" I said, "He did," which was true. On the other hand, Cataldo's girlfriend from Greenwich Village arrived at Cornell and made a pass at me: "Oooo you didn't tell me he was so CUTE!" I made a few trips to Greenwich Village, and that was that.

At the end of freshman year Cataldo "busted out" and the girl singer was on probation. Our band had been successful enough to make it necessary for me to join the Musicians' Union. Once we fronted for a showing of "stag movies" at an organization called Young Israel. They couldn't advertise the movies but they could advertise us. Everyone just walked past us as we played. Eventually we stopped playing and went downstairs to watch the movies ourselves.

The psychological pressures of college life are considerable, and there isn't space to deal with them here. Cornell had some interesting teachers—including, eventually, Paul de Man, who was a major influence on my understanding of criticism and on my view of Yeats. There was also an excellent course on Dante taught by Robert Durling, and I read Joyce's *Ulysses* in Arthur Mizener's course. (Mizener's take on *Ulysses* was rather conservative: "I want to emphasize the wonderful traditional novel that *Ulysses* really is." Not *Ulysses* as an experiment in liberated language.) I wrote considerably less poetry in college than I had in high school, partly because I was being asked to consider poetry *critically*, in ways that were not fully familiar to me. *What exactly did you mean by that? Was that put in only for the sound?*—as if that were some sort of terrible thing to do. Robert Durling was my freshman English teacher, and I would show him my poetry. I remember his description of my early work as "mellifluous Yeatsian vapidity." He smiled as he said it. But he said it. (I remember thinking that "Wolfian vapidity" might have been more accurate.)

For me the experience of poetry had been extraordinarily intense but utterly isolating. I had no way of knowing whether my work was any good, whether it "communicated." I had no one whose opinion I could really trust. To make matters worse, the opinions of most of my professors seemed to reflect those of the then-fashionable New Critics. For the New Critics, Shelley was a terrible poet. For me he was something like a god. (Whenever leaves show up in my poetry, Shelley's "Ode To The West Wind" is present.) Durling said to me, "Why did Shelley write, 'I die, I faint, I fail' in *that* order? How can you faint and fail *after* you have died?" I had no way of answering the question, though much later the *O.E.D.'s* article on "die" provided me with an excellent response: to die doesn't only mean to cease to exist; it means to swoon, to fall into a faint. "I die" in the sense of "I faint, I fail." I didn't find out about the *O.E.D.*, however, until long after I had left Cornell, when I came upon references to it in Robert Duncan's work. In many subtle ways I was encouraged to write criticism rather than poetry at Cornell, and I discovered that I was good at writing criticism. Like most college programs, Cornell's English Department tended to produce people who felt comfortable with analysis but uncomfortable with emotion—particularly with personal emotion.

I had hoped that Cornell would give me what I lacked in Port Chester, an intellectual community. It gave me something, but it didn't give me that. In my sophomore year I took a great many English courses. I wanted to learn everything at once. What I discovered was that, no matter the period or the writer, Chaucer or T.S. Eliot, the same kinds of questions were being raised, questions of irony, paradox, etc. This discovery made me realize that I wasn't in school to learn about literature. I was in school to learn a *grid* which could be applied to almost any piece of writing (though woe to the writer like Shelley to whom it *didn't* apply). This was a useful thing to learn, but it lessened the authority of my instructors.

When I read Thomas Gray's poem I believed (however inaccurately) that I had penetrated to the heart of poetry. I knew that Gray was a great writer because of the way he made me feel. I knew that Shelley was a great writer because of the way he made me feel. If my professors could not account for that feeling, their opinions didn't have to be taken too seriously. At the same time, however, I knew of no work which could further what I had already done. The poets I was reading were ones my professors approved of—or might approve of: Yeats, Eliot and Pound; Dylan Thomas, W.H. Auden, Robert Graves, Robert Lowell. Also Alan Dugan, George Starbuck, Arthur Freeman. John Crowe Ransom gave a charming reading and I acquired his *Selected Poems*. Robert Sward was teaching at Cornell at that time, and I knew him a little. I thought his book, *Uncle Dog*, was a delight. I missed Charles Olson's visit. (I heard from my friend Tom Hanna that Olson lamented the vanishing of the concept of Rhea—an important theme in his work. One of the professors said, "Oh, we have it in one word: *diar*rhea.") The writers I was reading influenced my verse, surely, but they could not push me forward, as Olson's work was to do some years later. At Cornell, I had no sense of direction. The closest I was able to come to such a sense was in something I wrote myself, a poem called "Orpheus" which was eventually published in *The Beloit Poetry Journal* in

1970, about eight years after it was written. The poem was influenced by Pound—particularly by "Moeurs Contemporaines" and "Mauberly," with their fragmented sections. Except for the opening lines, written as part of an earlier poem, it came all of a sudden, in a tremendous burst. It was as if the original poem suddenly decided to change direction and take on a life of its own. The central sections, including the somewhat homophobic lines about Whitman, were a deliberate echo of Lorca's *Poet In New York* and "Lament for Ignacio Sánchez Mejías:"

> Walt Whitman walks on the harbor, watching
> sea-gulls scatter, his beard full of lice.
> There he goes, with his body electric,
> chanting his chansons in the morning,
> never shaving.

> Walt eyes the sailors, with *their* bodies electric,
> electric to him, Walt Whitman,
> chanting his chants in the morning,
> never shaving.

> *

> Garcia Lorca chants Walt Whitman-
> Orpheus in the saddle,
> his beautiful eyes are gleaming.
> Never will there be an Andalusian
> as handsome as he.

> Now the worms eat him,
> now the worms chew up Garcia Lorca

> shot in the head for political reasons.

I realize now that the poem was telling me something about my own death and the death I sensed in my surroundings ("he goes on singing, singing / in a city run down by barbarians") but at the time I couldn't read it.

Here are three more poems from that period: "On The Ultimate Failure of Religiosity," "Love Song," and "Before Leaving Atlantic City." These three poems are more representative of what I was attempting than "Orpheus." The first suggests my uneasiness with both mother and mother church. The second suggests my sexual anxieties. (A woman said to me once, "I don't know whether you know it or not, but you have an absolutely terrific line!") I'll discuss the third poem in the next section. These poems show various influences, and they point towards my sense of poetry as something "physical," something even *dangerous* and *erotic*, though such words were hardly a description of my life.

ON THE ULTIMATE FAILURE OF RELIGIOSITY

The lineal direction of eternity
is not marked clearly.
Hansel-and-Gretel-like, I lose my way
and stumble into the wicked house
in the bewildering wood.
I had supposed that death was an accident,
a deviation from the usual path,
yet these sweet-toothed children
munching their gingerbread crumbs
in evident sensuality
are another matter.
They are content, untrue

to the fairy tale, awaiting
the inevitable movement
to the black pot stirred
by the old hag of the story,
and grateful for the compassionate act
of swift beaks snapping
umbilicus of usual bread.

*

LOVE SONG

This delicate piece of thread
proceeding by the longest possible route
from the point of my desire to your awareness—
had you postulated its existence,
I should have drawn it taut,
wound it easily on the spindle of
your acceptance,
but, as it is, must toss my line
hoping by some chance
you catch the baited inference.

Shall I remind you of its capacities?

Old tapestries,
diagrammatical pictures of the heart,
were woven by its ancestors,
and even the white surface of your indifference
might (with a bit of luck)
be rainbowed into passion by its working.

*

BEFORE LEAVING ATLANTIC CITY

The mother-sea exploded with a roar
before we put the lights out and it vanished.
Not even the ladies marching on the boardwalk

were storm enough to pull us down;
we rode out the daylight, dreaming
of drowsy islands where the water's calm.
Night was our harbor, when the midwife, love,
folded us in with its impossibilities,
fished out our pieces till the game made sense.
Sweetheart, forgive the liars and the fools
who shipped us to this place: they thought it best.
Sleep will bear you into gentler water
where painted characters of kings and castles
glitter like islands, and I will close your ears
to the disarranged palaver of pawns and landlubbers.

*

If you catch me stealin,' please don't tell on me.
    Lead Belly song

The third poem quoted, "Before Leaving Atlantic City," was written in December, 1961, as a love poem to my wife, Adelle. We had spent our honeymoon, at her parents' expense, in Atlantic City. I met Adelle through a complicated series of events.

I mentioned earlier that the pressures of college life are considerable: academic pressures, social pressures, issues of identity, sexuality, self-assertion. One is suddenly, willy nilly, ready or not, an "adult." In my case, I had never been away from home. I had never gone on a date. I had never received any instruction about sex. I remember my mother remarking to my father, "D"—short for Daddy, something from my infancy which stuck—"you ought to say something to him." Understanding exactly what she meant, my father parried the attack: "Nah," he said, "These days they tell them all about that in school." Then, turning to me, he added: "Don't they?" What could I say but "Yes"?

As a child I owned very few books (except for comic books, which were a great passion), and there were very few books in my house. If I wanted to read a book I got it out of the library. In my freshman English class at Cornell, I was assigned to do a report on Yeats' *A Vision*. I went to the teacher to explain that the book had been taken out of the library and so I couldn't do the report. He surprised me by saying, "Why don't you just buy the book?" The possibility of buying a book—any book—hadn't occurred to me. I bought the Yeats, did the report, and suddenly I was beginning to buy books. Unfortunately, my funds were extremely limited. Looking around me in a bookstore one day, I realized that it would be easy to *steal* a book. I reasoned that stealing a book or two from a university-owned bookstore was really harming no one, and, further, that I would use the books well, better than most of the people who had money to buy them. At that point I began to steal books in earnest, to set about building myself a library. Once, when a friend needed money, I stole a large law book from one book store and sold it at the other. Unfortunately, I didn't get enough money for it and I had to go back and steal still another law book! My stealing was not only illegal but self-expressive, a mode of subversive self-assertion in a situation in which I was constantly under the scrutiny of authority figures. Friends whom I told about it expressed admiration, though they didn't take up the trade themselves. Finally I stole books I didn't really need, would never get around to reading—though I prided myself on the fact that I never stole from libraries or independent bookstores.

Apparently, I was not alone in the activity of stealing. There were articles in the Cornell paper about the increase in book-stealing, and the bookstores began to install anti-theft devices. One of the stores featured a "plainclothes" guard, who was supposed to blend in with the students. He didn't blend in. During one of my expeditions I realized that he was watching me. I decided to give him something to watch. I picked up more and more books and carried them around the store with me. I knew I could put these books on my credit account and get away. It would be expensive, but I wouldn't be accused of stealing. I remember thinking that the guard was probably wondering whether I would do that. I walked over to the clerk as if I were going to pay for the books, chatted with him for a few moments, and then—walked out the door. As soon as my foot was outside, a hand was on my shoulder. I handed over the books and, later, a few others from my library. I argued that I had read about the increase in stealing and, since I had little money, thought I could steal a few books too. I was put on suspension for a year. Someone remarked, "You seem almost relieved." Robert Langbaum, one of my teachers, said, "I hope you realize you've done a horrible thing." "There was," as the French Lieutenant's Woman says to her ex-lover in both book and movie, "a wildness in me at that time." The relief my friend noticed was real. Stealing books was a way of extricating myself from an increasingly unbearable situation, and of doing so without the pain of a direct confrontation. Did I wish to stay in school? Was Cornell the right place for me? I needed time off but had no way to ask for it. Stealing deflected my attention from those difficult questions and, finally, provided me with time. When my parents learned of my suspension they rose to the occasion admirably—my mother had after all been caught doing the same thing—and I was welcomed home.

Several years earlier, my mother had sued, or threatened to sue, our landlord when I accidentally pushed my hand through a pane of glass on the front door to the apartment house. The injury issued in a panicked trip to the hospital and a fairly obvious scar on my left arm. My mother argued that the scar might mar my career in show business (not that I had a career in show business), and the landlord gave her some money. This money had been put aside for me to use as I wished. I had recently gone to Boston to see a Cornell friend, Giancarlo Buzzi, before he went home to Italy. I decided it might be nice to spend the summer of 1960 in Cambridge. I tried finding jobs in the Boston area but none of them worked out. Finally, at my mother's suggestion, I took advantage of my savings. The money allowed me not only to live in Cambridge but to attend Harvard Summer School.

In Cambridge I acquired a whole new set of friends. Moreover, I discovered that it was not unfashionable to be a writer/thief. Jean Genet was at the height of his fame. So my petty thievery tended to work to my advantage. One of the people I met, Lewis H. Rubman, changed the course of my life. Rubman was amazing. He had a mustache, for one thing. For another, he had a car. Furthermore, he was extremely frank about sex—and he had some of those beautiful Henry Miller books published by Olympia Press in Paris. His parents were well off (he was an inhabitant of that middle class I both envied and disdained) and he had actually undergone some psychotherapy. He was, I believe, looking for a best friend, a best friend for life, and he sensed that in me. Neither of us was writing very much but there was always a good deal of intellectual excitement. One of the courses I was taking included the magnificent Brecht/Weill opera, *Aufstieg Und Fall der Stadt Mahagonny.* I listened to the record over and over. Brecht's play, with its self-conscious "bits," suggested a new and, to me, astonishing direction for *vaudeville*. Later, I translated Brecht's lyric to "Surabaya Johnny," only to discover that the lyric was itself a translation of Kipling's poem, "Mary, Pity Women." It was a marvelous summer.

When the summer was over, Rubman returned to New York City, where he was going to NYU. He had an apartment on East 11th Street. I went back to Port Chester. Arguments with my parents increased. My father was terrified that he would have to support me for life. Finally, over my parents' fierce objections (my mother writhing on the floor, my father shouting, "You're killing that woman!"), I moved into a rooming house not far away from home.

I got a job as a bank teller and, for the first time in my life, was able to support myself. I felt that if my parents were going to make my life miserable, there was no reason I had to stay with them. My bank teller job meant that my father didn't have to give me any money. What did my parents have to give me if they could no longer give me money? My difficulties with my mother remained unresolved when she died in 1964. I walked out of the hospital and burst into tears. During our deathwatch over her, however, my father and I were able to feel close to one another again. When he died three years later, I felt that we had arrived at some sort of understanding.

Moving out of the house meant I could do what I liked with my time. Every second weekend I visited Rubman in New York. The other weekends he drove to Goucher College in Maryland, where a woman he'd met in Cambridge, Ellen, was going to school. I accompanied him a few times. On one of these trips he introduced me to his old friend Adelle, whom he'd known in elementary school and whom I would soon marry. He had been recently re-introduced to her by Ellen, and he'd been very impressed. "She's read *Finnegans Wake*," he told me. Adelle had not only read *Finnegans Wake*, she had lived abroad for a year; her French was better than mine. Since she was an economics major and good at math some friends wondered whether we could find anything to talk about. Some, such as Mike Abrams' mother, even advised vehemently against the relationship. I remember Mike saying over and over again, "Listen to her, man, she knows." But Adelle and I weren't experiencing any problems.

As my relationship with my own family deteriorated, Adelle's family welcomed me. I spent the next summer in New York City—my father was able to get me a job in a Western Union office in Bowling Green—and I saw a great deal of Adelle and her parents. Adelle and I were almost exactly the same age (I was 6 days older) but she had skipped a grade, so she was a year ahead of me. After graduation from Goucher, she entered graduate school at Cornell. We lived together for a short time and were married in Foley Square in New York City on December 21, 1961, the longest night of the year. I did not know at that time that Foley Square had been named for my father's father. I cursorily invited my parents to the wedding. My mother, rightly, was insulted, and they didn't attend. My best man was Lewis Rubman.

My mother would not have been happy had I married anyone, I think. At the same time she realized that I was threatening to break off relations with her and my father entirely. I had a deep need for family and, at the same time, a deep need to break away from family. But—like my father—I was discovering that it was possible, at least in part, to substitute one family for another. Adelle's parents accepted me without question. Their kindness and understanding are things I will always be grateful for.

At Cornell my writing tended to focus on song lyrics. Warren Wechsler, a classmate, wrote charming songs and played piano. We began to collaborate: I provided lyrics, Warren provided music. Finally we found people willing to write a libretto and we put on an original musical, *Tom Jones*. I sang one of the songs and worked out a tap dance. Adelle had a brief role—she played a servant girl who initiates the action by leaving baby Tom at the front door—and she handled the finances. The musical was a success, and we were asked to stage it again for a big weekend at the end of the year. Had I not been suspended, 1962 would have been my senior year. I produced a poem, "Tunnel of Love," which was at once a love poem and a good-bye to all that:

> Hard-put by the weather,
> we await the spring
> in sluggish Ithaca.
> Stuck
> in a ramshackle town,
> I love you up to keep the blankets warm.
>
> Back home,
> the foghorns bellow in the dingy harbor
> while mother putters at her indoor plants.
> They are the household deities:
> anchored,
> they flower in a bad season
> while the crazy tugs
> teeter and totter in a choppy sea.
>
> Broken by winter,
> we huddle mole-like in the covers,
>
> two old sailors
> blindly anchored in our Tunnel of Love.

*

This one was one very many were knowing some
and very many were glad to meet him, very many
sometimes listened to him, some listened to him very
often, there were some who listened to him, and he
talked then and he told them then that certainly he
had been one suffering and he was then being one
trying to be certain that he was wrong in doing what
he was doing and he had come then to be certain that
he never would be certain that he was doing what it
was wrong for him to be doing then and he was
suffering then and he was certain that he would be
one doing what he was doing and he was certain that
he should be one doing what he was doing and he
was certain that he would always be one suffering
and this then made him certain this, that he would
always be one being suffering, this made him certain
that he was expressing something being struggling....
Gertrude Stein, "Matisse"

In 1963 Adelle and I were heading west, on our way to
Berkeley, California. I had been awarded a Woodrow Wilson
Fellowship; Adelle was soon to find a job at the Federal Reserve
Bank of San Francisco. Interestingly, the job was arranged by the
radical economist, Douglas Dowd, with whom Adelle had studied
at Cornell. Paul de Man good-naturedly told me that I had better get
my tennis game together because that's all anyone did in Berkeley.
In 1962 I had finally learned to drive. We purchased a 1956
Oldsmobile to make the trip across country. Two close friends, Mike
Lurie, whom I had met in Cambridge, and Ed Pechter, were already

living in Berkeley. Then Rubman surprised us by showing up to live there too. We found an apartment without much trouble. The following year we found a place in Oakland; ten years later we bought a house in Oakland. We lived in that house together until Adelle's death in 2016.

I used to tell a story: In 1963, when I decided to move from Ithaca, New York, where I had been an undergraduate at Cornell, to attend graduate school in Berkeley, California, the smartest person I knew—the critic, Paul de Man—told me that I had better get my tennis game together because that's all anybody did in Berkeley. De Man went on to speak of one of his students: "She writes criticism the way she plays tennis: not always accurate but lots of enthusiasm." As he spoke of the student, he swung his arm as if playing tennis. I remembered his remark and his bemused noting of a connection between two rather disparate things—tennis and literary criticism—when I read that, dying of cancer, he wrote to Jacques Derrida that the French word, *tumeur* (tumor) sounded exactly like *"tu meurs"* (you—intimate form—die). If there was a slight hint of sexual interest in the woman he played tennis with, who came to mind at the mention of Berkeley, there was a bemused recognition of his own death when he thought of the word, *tumeur* and its punning relationship to his situation. De Man went on to become both famous and, later, notorious, and I tested my newly acquired skill of driving as we crossed the country, visiting friends, seeing things we had never seen before, going west. I remember noting that every day, towards the end of the day, the sun was in my eyes.

The Free Speech Movement (The FSM) happened in 1964, about a year after I arrived in Berkeley. It was (*Wikipedia*) a "massive, long-lasting student protest which took place during the 1964–65 academic year on the campus of the University of California, Berkeley...With the participation of thousands of students, the Free Speech Movement was the first mass act of civil disobedience on an American college campus in the 1960s." But De Man was not entirely wrong. Adelle and I moved into an apartment on McGee—2338, if I remember correctly—and the landlord and landlady were tennis enthusiasts who often wore their white tennis outfits around the house. I remember being told that the Hotel Claremont was a bastion of "the old Berkeley"—and of course of tennis. I remember as well a "radical bookstore" run by an Irishman named Farrell on was it Dwight Way—which a friend used to pronounce in the Chaucerian fashion: "Dwicht Why." Adelle, amused by that, pronounced it that way every chance she got. And Farrell told me that his mother, like my father, had been in vaudeville. I believe he dyed his hair red to emphasize both his political beliefs and his Irishness. And of course to appear younger than he was.

In Berkeley my writing stopped almost entirely as I concentrated on graduate school or participated in that explosion of energy we call "the sixties." In Berkeley, Lewis Rubman lived in an apartment building where Mario Savio's then girlfriend, later wife, still later ex wife, was also living; I believe both the girlfriend and Rubman hailed from Westport, Connecticut, and had known each other there. Since Rubman knew many of the people involved with The Free Speech Movement, I got to meet them early on. I protested the war with them—though I never officially joined the FSM—and I experimented with LSD and marijuana. (I deliberately took acid *before* I took marijuana so that no one could accuse me of "going on to the harder stuff.") I learned rock songs and played them on my electric guitar. Until that time my guitar playing had depended entirely on sheet music. I now learned to trust (and develop) my ear. Berkeley radio station KPFA broadcast an astonishing range of art programming, which I found fascinating. I had read Alan Watts on religion, but here he was actually speaking. Here, Jaime de Angulo's Basque accent was delivering marvelous Native American "Old Time Stories." I first heard Gertrude Stein's voice on KPFA; I was enthralled and somewhat surprised to discover that I understood her! During this time, a short poem written in Berkeley while I worked for The Cinema Guild, "The Skeleton's Defense of Carnality," was published in *The Beloit Poetry Journal*. I was managing the Guild Theater on Telegraph, and the poem was written in a ticket booth during a lull. I could hear the people inside the theater enjoying the film while I had to remain outside, in the ticket booth. I was perhaps feeling particularly sorry for myself because Adelle and I had briefly split up and were experimenting with living apart from one another.

Later we both agreed that the split was a bad idea, which was probably what my poem was telling me, too.

THE SKELETON'S DEFENSE OF CARNALITY

Truly I have lost weight, I *have*
Lost weight,
Grown lean in love's defense,
In love's defense grown grave.
It was concupiscence
That brought me to the state:
All bone and a bit of skin
To keep the bone within.

Flesh is no heavy burden
For one possessed of little
And accustomed to its loss.
I lean to love, which leaves me lean
Till lean turn into lack.

A wanton bone, I sing my song
And travel where the bone is blown
And extricate true love from lust
As any man of wisdom must.

Then wherefore should I rage
Against this pilgrimage
From gravel unto gravel?
Circuitous I travel
From love to lack
And lack to lack,
From lean to lack
And back.

Words like "concupiscence" and "circuitous" attest to my having recently read John Crowe Ransom's excellent essay on

Shakespeare's use of Latinate words. Ransom himself was capable of lines like "Declension looks from our land, it is old" ("Antique Harvesters"). My poem was later inscribed on a tile in Berkeley as part of The Addison Street Project, though, unfortunately, the lines beginning, "Then wherefore should I rage" were accidentally omitted from the tile—making the poem rather more positive than it is. The poem is correctly printed in the book that accompanied The Addison Street Project. I used to show the tile to people, recite the poem in its entirety, and do a brief tap dance on the tile.

A paper written for Stanley Fish's excellent Milton course at Berkeley was published in the prestigious journal, *ELH*. I was amused when Mr. Fish asked me whether I knew what a phenomenologist was. "I have been called a phenomenologist," he explained. I knew and informed him. "Oh," he said. "It's good to know what you are." I enjoyed many of the courses I was taking. But the basic story of my life in the sixties and seventies is my increasing awareness that I *could not be* a member of the academy. There were constant tensions between my personal vision and what was acceptable in graduate school. At one point I produced a long, complicated paper on "Holy Thursday" for a seminar on Blake. The paper went over like a lead balloon, but twenty years later a long, Joycean passage from it found its way into my poem, "Fifty":

WE HAVE HERE—AS WE HAVE AT THE CONCLUSION OF "THE ECHOING GREEN"—A KIND OF GRADUAL FADING OF THE LIGHT IN WHICH THINGS ARE NO LONGER SEEN

CLEARLY AND IN WHICH THE SOUNDS WE "HEAR" TEND
TO BECOME SOMEWHAT DISTANT: "ALL THE HILLS
ECHOED." AT THIS POINT, I THINK, LANGUAGE BECOMES
SOMETHING CLOSE TO PURE POTENTIALITY, TO PURE
"SOUND" OR "MUSIC," TO THE "SONG" THAT THE PIPER
PIPES. WHAT BLAKE IS ATTEMPTING TO MAKE US DO, I
SUSPECT, IS TO TREAT *ALL* OF HIS WORDS IN THE SAME
WAY THAT WE MUST TREAT THE NAMES OF HIS
CHARACTERS: WE MUST CONTINUALLY RECOMBINE
THEM, MUST TURN THEM AROUND AND AROUND IN OUR
MINDS UNTIL THEY BECOME WORDS WHICH, THOUGH
DIFFERENT, INVOLVING OTHER LETTERS, RETAIN IN
THEIR SOUNDS THE ECHOES OF ONE ANOTHER. BLAKE
HIMSELF USED WORDS OF THE BIBLE IN ORDER TO
CREATE   NEW   HARMONIES,   HARMONIES   WHICH
"CHIMED" WITH THOSE OF THE BIBLE, AND I THINK
"HOLY THURSDAY" WAS MEANT TO SERVE THE SAME
PURPOSE. TWAS ON A, FOR EXAMPLE, MIGHT EASILY
BECOME TWAS HONOR, HOSANNA; THE SEATS OF
HEAVEN, THE SAINTS OF HEAVEN, THE SEEDS OF
HEAVEN; BENEATH THEM SIT, BE NEATH THEM SAID;
WHITE AS SNOW, WHY 'TIS SNOW, WHY 'TIS NOW; TILL
INTO, TELL UNTO, TOLL UNTO; THE VOICE OF SONG,
THEY VOICE HIS SONG, THEIR VOICE IS SONG, THEIR
VOICE, HIS SONG; THE FLOWERS OF LONDON TOWN, OR
LAND ATONED, OR LENTEN TIME; BUT MULTITUDES OF
LAMBS, BUT MULTITUDES OF LANDS, BUT MULTITUDES
OF   LIMBS,   BOUGHT   MULTITUDES   OF   LAMBS;
THOUSANDS OF LITTLE BOYS, THOSE SANDS OF LITTLE
BOYS; O WHAT A, O WATER; THE HUM OF MULTITUDES,
THE HOME OF MULTITUDES, THE HYMN, THE HAM, THE
HIM OF MULTITUDES; THEY LIKE THAMES WATERS
FLOW, THEY LIGHT TIME'S WATERS FLOW, THEIR
NIGHTTIMES WATERS FLOW; RADIANCE ALL THEIR
OWN, RADIANCE ALL THEREROUND, RADIANCE ALL
THEREON, REGENTS ARE THERE CROWNED; THE
CHILDREN WALKING, THE CAULDRON WAKING, THE

CALLED ARE WALKING; HARMONIOUS THUNDERINGS, OUR MOAN, HIS THUNDERINGS; THE VOICE, THE VOWS, THE JOYS.

My experience as manager of the Guild was also of some interest. The Guild was part of a conglomerate of three theaters: The Cinema on Shattuck Avenue, The Guild and the smaller theater, The Studio, located next to The Guild on Telegraph Avenue. Together, they were called The Cinema Guild. None of these theaters could be called the last word in theatrical amenities. Joseph Kramer, one of my professors at UC Berkeley, used to refer to the Studio as "The Rat Trap." But they showed great films, both international and American. I knew that the film critic Pauline Kael had made her name writing program notes for these theaters as well as by broadcasting on KPFA. She had recently divorced her husband, Ed Landberg, who owned the theaters, and after the divorce she had headed for the East Coast to make what would be a very successful career for herself. In addition to Landberg, she had been married to someone who later became a dear friend of mine: the filmmaker/poet, James Broughton. Their relationship was sometimes difficult because she wished him to become a mainstream Hollywood filmmaker, something that the bohemian Broughton had no wish to be. I believe they parted amicably, but Kael's divorce from Landberg was evidently rather acrimonious: her last program note read, "Leaving because of a dispute with the management." Landberg tried to gather up all the copies of that note but he didn't succeed.

It was my job as manager to find Kael's notes about a particular film Landberg was showing; if she hadn't written anything, I had to provide something. Ed Landberg also instructed me in "walking the ladder"—balancing yourself precariously on a ladder as you changed the lettering on the theater marquis. He was a strange, somewhat pompous man who spoke with a rather odd accent that emphasized individual words. Each word he said seemed to indicate "I am important: listen to me." He invited me to dinner with his then wife, Roz, and explained that he and Roz were basically "writers." He showed me a brief piece he had written— saying it contained "everything he knew about women"—but I didn't find the piece very impressive. I was later told that Roz "took him for everything he had" when, like Kael, she divorced him. Despite Landberg's rocky personal relations, the Cinema Guild showed marvelous films, and those films offered everyone an education in that deeply engaging, complex twentieth-century art form. Later, the Pacific Film Archive at UC Berkeley took up the same task. I learned much from both. (I was in the Pacific Film Archive watching a Fritz Lang film on the night that Fritz Lang died.)

Some of my friends referred to Ed Landberg as "slimy" or "creepy." I saw this in action once. He was more or less coming on to a young woman, another of his employees. I don't remember what the young woman said but he answered it, chuckling, with "Oh, how sweet and virginal of you." I was annoyed at his insinuating tone and said to the woman, "Are you a virgin?" She answered angrily, "That's none of your business!" She later thanked me for what I had done. She couldn't be angry at him: he could have fired her. But she could be angry at me. In his later years, Landberg went mad in a rather gentle and unthreatening way. He believed himself to be Jesus—or, at any rate, The Messiah. His madness was elaborated into a complex fiction in which he was to mate with Joan Baez and thus produce the end of the world. He would discuss this madness in a very rational way: "If I am who I think I am...." His problem was that he had no way to contact Joan Baez. He decided that she would immediately fall in love with him if only she could hear him. He rented a hall in Oakland and read his poetry there. No one came. He asked me to do a radio show with him. I did. There is no evidence that Joan Baez ever heard it. Once, I told James Broughton that I knew someone who believed himself to be The Messiah. Broughton, who sometimes had his own problems with fantasy, answered seriously, "I *know* I'm The Messiah." When I told Ed Landberg about this conversation, he became very agitated and asked, "Is he Jewish?" I answered, "No." Landberg breathed a sigh of relief.

I had hoped that Cornell would provide me with an intellectual community. It did not. My experience at Berkeley was similar, though again there were moments of excitement. Josephine Miles, Joseph Kramer, Paul Alpers, and others taught courses which interested me though there was no one there of the quality and charisma of Paul de Man. Henry Nash Smith's course included Charles Feidelson, Jr.'s excellent book, *Symbolism And American Literature*, with its intriguing discussions of Melville, Poe and Whitman. A 1971 class taught by James Breslin introduced me to many writers whom I had previously neglected, particularly to William Carlos Williams, whose masterly *Spring and All* was on the reading list. We also read Robert Duncan's magnificent *Bending the Bow*. (I had bought Duncan's *Selected Poems* in Ithaca and been fascinated by "The Venice Poem" and "Homage to the Brothers Grimm.") Duncan lived in San Francisco and often gave lectures and readings. On a particularly memorable occasion during a talk given at the university, his mind drifted off between Shakespeare's *Romeo and Juliet* and Jack Spicer, and as he spoke of Spicer, he began to weep. I saw him frequently in Berkeley going to the bookstores or the library. There were also writers—poets—in Breslin's class: Paul Lobo Portugés was part of the class; Ron Silliman, David Melnick and Rochelle Nameroff had all recently published books through a press called "Ithaca House," located, ironically enough, at Cornell, though I had known nothing of it during my time at the university. Further, James Breslin was the judge of Berkeley's Yang Poetry Prize that year, and a little selection of my poems was one of the winners. Still, I could hardly call myself a writer. By 1970 I was really nothing more than a professional graduate student.

On April 5, 1970, at the age of twenty-nine, I gave up smoking. On May 6 of that year I began a journal: "What do I want to come of this? Some self-knowledge. I have been a propagandist for self-knowledge. I really know very little of myself."

By 1974 I had finally had enough of graduate school. I made a last-ditch effort to write a PhD thesis. A long paper on Shakespeare's *Cymbeline*, written for Joseph Kramer's class, might be the basis of a thesis. The only problem with the paper was that it didn't mention a single critic. I set about to remedy that. The books I needed were sometimes taken out of the main library. In the undergraduate library, however, there was a set of stacks which had just about everything. Nobody ever touched it. Unfortunately, as I read the critics I found myself getting angry. *Cymbeline* was not a play which anyone seemed to have understood very well. Even people whose work I usually liked had little of interest to say about it. The problem was partly historical. It was fairly common knowledge in Shakespeare's time that Cymbeline's reign coincided with the birth of Christ. This unmentioned fact colors the entire play as its Pagan characters—with no knowledge of Christ—begin to act like Christians. None of the critics I was reading had any awareness of this important aspect of the play. Finally, I got up and wandered over to the modern poetry section. There I came upon Charles Olson's *Maximus IV V VI*. I found the book amazing. I'm not sure I understood it in the usual sense in which one "understands" things. On the other hand, I understood it. *Maximus IV V VI*, with its size, its ample white space, its *freedom* was a revelation, or, as Jake Berry said about another book, a baptism. I went back and forth between the critics and Olson until I realized that I was in fact acting out a little psychodrama. Do you want to be *this* (critic) or do you want to be *this* (Olson)? The decision was obvious. I left school. I wanted to be Olson.

Leaving school freed me towards reading again. I plunged into Gertrude Stein and Pound's *Cantos*, both stunning experiences. Like Robert Kelly as he tells it in *A Controversy of Poets*, I felt transformed by Williams' astonishing "Asphodel, That Greeny Flower." I read the Beats with better understanding than ever before. L=A=N=G=U=A=G=E poets were just beginning to publish, and I was aware of their work. Ron Silliman, whom I knew through James Breslin's class, was prominent in that movement. A KPFA program introduced me to Jack Kerouac's marvelous reading style. I read all the Duncan I could find. Michael McClure's essay, "Phi Upsilon Kappa," opened his work to me ("Writing this is a kind of pain as well as a joy at the chance to make a new liberty"). KPFA broadcast an extraordinary production of Antonin Artaud's radio play, *Pour En Finir Avec Le Jugement De Dieu* (*To End God's Judgment*) which included both a marvelous translation of Artaud's work by Victor Corti, performed by San Francisco Actor's Workshop, and an acoustic version featuring Artaud himself, whose cries, mutterings and screeches were astonishing. I immediately hunted up *The Theater and Its Double*. I also read Louis Zukofsky, Jack Spicer,

Larry Eigner, H.D., Amiri Baraka, Langston Hughes, Clayton Eshleman (a wonderful poem on Charlie Parker), Zora Neale Hurston, and local California poets Ishmael Reed, Brother Antonius, Victor Hernandez Cruz, Al Young, Edward Mycue, Diane di Prima, and Adrienne Rich. Through Rich I came upon Judy Grahn's stunning poem, *A Woman Is Talking To Death* and then her later poetry and her wonderful essays. Walter J. Ong's work became an endless source of inspiration and insight. Books like *The Autobiography of Malcolm X*, Jean Toomer's *Cain*, and W.E.B. Du Bois's *The Souls of Black Folks*—to say nothing of Ishmael Reed's great novel, *Mumbo Jumbo*—opened my eyes to African-American experience. The Before Columbus Foundation showed me the great range and beauty of what we designate as "ethnic" writing. Jerome Rothenberg's marvelous anthologies and his excellent verse opened up new possibilities of poetic expression which, paradoxically, were rooted in ancient practices. Gregory Bateson—whom I saw give a lecture at the university—taught me a good deal, as did Carl Sauer, whose work I discovered through Olson. I explored the occult: A.E. Waite, Aleister Crowley, Max Heindel, Corinne Heline—the latter two Southern Californians. (Heline's little book on the moon in occult lore is masterly.) I finally read Heidegger, to whom Paul de Man was always referring. *Sein und Zeit*, recently translated into English as *Being and Time*, was a life-changing experience, clarifying things that had previously been opaque, even unknown. Later, it occurred to me that Heidegger's argument that "world" was always and necessarily an aspect of *Dasein* (Heidegger's term for specifically human being, literally "being there": *da* + *sein*) might suggest that "performance" could be understood as an aspect of the supposedly "inward" act of writing poetry: inward and outward, subjective and objective, self and world were not opposites so much as constant elements, tensions within a process that could be reduced to neither one separately. *Dasein* was not an entity, not an I, but a process, a movement. In the course of *Being and Time*'s massive, fascinating arguments and its experiments with language, the book presented me with an experience of death so deeply "private," so "subjective," so "individual" that it could scarcely find words. But Heidegger had deliberately excluded words like "private," "subjective," "individual" from his philosophical vocabulary. Even here, in this most "inward," most "subjective" of states, "world"— the "outer"—was a necessary aspect of the experience being named. Couldn't that insight, the notion that world was always an aspect of "inwardness," be used to think about "performance poetry"? Wasn't all poetry in some sense "performance poetry"—inward, yes, but also necessarily involving *world*, a word which might be extended to *performance*, which takes place in world.

Years later, I connected this insight to Walt Whitman's great phrase, "Death's outlet song of life" ("When Lilacs Last in the Dooryard Bloom'd"). The deep experience of the death of my wife Adelle somehow created in me a blossoming of language: death and life, inner and outer, a heartbreaking private event which was also a public event, all closely intertwined.

I also read Wittgenstein, Gurdjieff, Whitehead, Freud, Nietzsche, Jung, and Foucault, whose *History of Sexuality, Part One* taught me something about laughter in philosophy. Hannah Arendt's *The Human Condition*—brilliant and deeply influenced by Heidegger—was read and re-read, along with others of her books. Her understanding of freedom was not the great American experience of separating oneself from others (leaving the womb) but the experience of encountering others in what she thought of as a theater: freedom was *political, social,* as much as it was the creation of "the individual."

Partly through the good offices of Charles Amirkhanian at KPFA, I was listening to experimental music as well as reading experimental poetry. Charles Ives' *Concord Sonata* and his book, *Essays Before A Sonata* were enormous influences, as were his songs. I first heard Lou Harrison on KPFA and was able to attend several of his concerts at near-by Mills College. I had acquired Kenneth Rexroth's wonderful edition of D.H. Lawrence's poetry in Ithaca. Now I was reading Rexroth's poetry and listening to him on KPFA. My friend Ed Michel gave me a collection of records he had produced, so I began with great excitement to listen seriously to jazz. Eisenstein's essays were also tremendously exciting, as was Abel Gance's marvelous "polyvision" film, *Napoleon*, which Adelle and I saw at The Avenue Theater in San Francisco. I haunted UC

Berkeley's Pacific Film Archive and, centering on Alfred Hitchcock, published a few essays on film. (Gary Morris, the editor of *Bright Lights* magazine, was a constant supporter of my work in this area.) I began to think seriously about the art of painting. Clyfford Still's abstractions fascinated me. A 1977 exhibition of Jess's work at the UC Berkeley University Art Museum had an enormous impact. Through Jess, whom I was later to know as a friend, I discovered Max Ernst and all the people to whom Jess referred in his multilayered paintings. Kandinsky's paintings and his book, *Concerning The Spiritual In Art*, were powerful expressions that opened me further to the possibilities of art not as mimetic or self-expressive but as revelatory—something that brought you into the presence of another "world," something you barely knew existed. Isn't that what happened to me when I read Thomas Gray? Wasn't astonishment an aspect of the highest art? Wasn't Shakespeare's work a constant revelation of astonishment? Etc.

My poetry was, however, to use Gertrude Stein's word, still "struggling." Under the influence of Breslin's course and its participants I began to produce a kind of experimental verse. Remembering both Paul Valéry and a brand of candy, I put these poems together in a short sequence called "Charmes." Each of the poems was an ecstatic, only partially understood experience, though they all centered in a word or words that were simultaneously nouns and verbs. Here is the third:

randy belly . look & come . there are clouds in the-

                            .

            hardly the ice . ends

                            .

                    folding   lines
                    quiet is the

                            .

                    cross-ing the
                    crossing   toss-
                        crossed

Such poems were wonderful when they came, but they were few and far between. Though the poems seemed to celebrate my entrance into the ecstatic state in which poetry was possible ("crossing the / crossing toss- / crossed"), I had no idea how that state might be induced or how in fact I had fallen into it.

                            *

            Immature poets imitate; mature poets steal.
                    —T.S. Eliot, "Philip Massinger"

        ...

COMME SI
Even if you have no audience, you must proceed
as if you had one.
                    —Jack Foley

On June 25, 1974 I was utterly depressed about my writing. I had just brought our car in for servicing—never a happy obligation—and taken the bus back home. I was extremely tired and believed at that moment I would never produce anything of any value. My life as a poet seemed to have ended. Glancing at a collection of Charles Olson's essays—particularly at "Human Universe"—I noticed a sentence which began, "If there is any truth at all to the idea that...." Certain that nothing would come of it, I typed on a piece of paper, "If there is any truth at all" and added, as if in commentary, "(there is)". I went on to appropriate others of Olson's phrases, changing them if I felt like it. (Olson actually wrote, "It is *not* the Greeks I blame.")

> if there is any truth at all (there is)
> it is the greeks I blame
> the lines in which
>   speech takes place
> & Melville did....

Next I took a recent passage from my journal,

>   a waking dream.
> Someone (me, not me) on a rooftop. Being chased?
>   Crowds. The man's friends below, holding a
> net which looks like an awning, urge him.
>   Tremendous distance!
> The man jumps!—he misses the awning.
> I remark (it is remarked to me): he didn't check
>   which way the wind was blowing,

and retyped it, moving my fingers slightly so I would hit some of the wrong keys and leaving out some of it, revising as I went along:

> a wajubg dreanL
> sineibe OOne.bitg neOOib a riiftioOObeubg cgased.
> Criwds the man's friends bekiw
> gikdubg a bet kiijs kuje ab wawbubg 'greeb
>   tremendous distance
> yrge
>   urge him
>
>   to killowatts

My depression vanished. The poem suddenly came alive, "the urge to kill" becoming "the urge to *killowatts*," to energy. Its seemingly obvious discovery that literature was made out of *letters* was extraordinarily liberating, and its concluding lines, only half-understood when I wrote them, "the page is not the / natural dividing point," thrust me into an entirely new direction. A sequence of such poems followed. I called it "Letters" and dedicated it to "the sixth Marx brother: Typo." (Olson's praise of the typewriter in his famous essay, "Projective Verse," was undoubtedly in the back of my mind.) Then a friend, Richard Segasture, sent me his play, *Limbo*. I thought it might be interesting to include what I called "Choruses"—theater pieces—in his play, and he agreed. The first of these was later published in my book, *Adrift*. Its opening line is a kind of stage direction:

Darkness. The light comes slowly.

What is it?
It sweetens the circulation of the blood.
My blood is circular enough already.
And your reasoning?
What is it?
Voices.   Voices.

The piece goes on to quote from Darwin, Einstein, Hans Christian Andersen, W.H. Prescott, and others. Writing another of these choruses, I decided to involve Adelle in its performance. The first chorus moved through various voices, but I could perform it solo. With two speakers, voices could be thrust against one another, simultaneously (Ives!). I worked out the poem's timing by using a tape recording of my own voice, then presented it to Adelle. We became very interested in the possibilities of the form. Thinking partly of its placement in Segasture's play but also regarding it as a genuine "opening," I named the poem "Overture." It became the "Words For Adelle" of my first book, *Letters/Lights—Words For Adelle*:

that the hummingbird's wings are of a remarkable rapidity
he had noted often
        nothing could be done   the shift of his breathing   had
        to begin
12 o'clock and he still hadn't had a   dermal sensation

Such poems were tremendously exciting, but, apart from Adelle, I had no audience and no idea where to present my work.

An acquaintance invited me to an open poetry reading in Berkeley. I didn't read anything, but he tried to read a long poem which he regarded as the best thing he had written. The mc, Paladin, decided he was going on too long and ran him off the stage. "I want to finish," he said. All the lights went out and when they came back on he was pulled off the stage. I had begun to write long poems too, so I was not encouraged to present my work there, though I had been sitting next to Berkeley's poet/"Bubble Lady," Julia Vinograd and she had been quite friendly. "Overture" was performed at someone's birthday party in 1974. It was well received, but it wasn't performed again until 1985, when Adelle and I gave our first reading. My isolation had allowed me to develop a kind of poetry which I found immensely satisfying. At the same time, however, there was absolutely no one to validate it. My friend from Cambridge and Berkeley, Mike Lurie, would make occasional comments about my work, but he was the only person to do so. He was hit by an automobile in New Jersey and killed. I remember thinking, in the midst of my grief, "Now there is no one to read my work!"

Not that I had much time to mope over the fate of my writing. On February 20, 1974, Adelle gave birth to a son, whom we named Sean Ezra, Sean a version of my name and my father's and Ezra after Pound and Ezra Cornell, who had indirectly furnished me with a ticket to college. Sean, someone quipped, had been *exFoliated*. The presence of a son was a great joy, the occasion of stories, humor, even of the creation of an imaginary creature named by Sean "The

D D D Monster." Though "The Monst" *looked* like me, he had a separate history. He *sounded* a little like Sean as a baby. Later came the arrival of a female creature called "The E E E Monster." *She* looked like Adelle and featured speech made up entirely of e's.

For the next several years I was a househusband, taking care of Sean, bringing him to school, etc. Ed Pechter moved to Canada to teach and Lewis Rubman and I became utterly estranged. Friends left and new friends appeared. We got to know other parents.

Meeting poet Iván Argüelles in 1985 changed almost everything.

I had known Iván's wife, Marilla, because she taught at Sean's elementary school, Park Day School in Oakland. I also knew that Iván was a widely-published poet, but I hadn't read much of his poetry. I ran into Marilla at a party given by an old friend of Adelle's mother. I had recently gotten to know Ishmael Reed, whose daughter, Tennessee, was attending Park Day. I mentioned Ishmael to Marilla, who told me that Iván might be interested in meeting him. I said, "Maybe I can arrange that," and was introduced to Iván, who gave me two of his books to read. "Let me know what you think of them," he said. I thought they were wonderful. Here was an extraordinary, wildly visionary, wildly funny work, full of pain yet full of comedy as well. I wrote Iván a long letter about his poetry. Later he told me the letter came closer to what he felt his poetry was like than anything he'd ever received before. He also said he was going to be reading at the Larry Blake's series in Berkeley. "You mention that you write. Why don't you read with me? If your poetry is even half as good as your criticism, you'll be fine." I learned later that such generosity was characteristic of this amazing man.

As it happened, the Native American writer Gerald Vizenor, whom I knew through a course sponsored by Ishmael Reed's Before Columbus Foundation, was also about to do a poetry reading. Gerry's reading was to be at The California College of Arts and Crafts in Oakland. I told him about my upcoming reading with Iván and he suggested that I read with him as well. The organizer of Gerry's reading phoned me asking whether I would like to be on for a half hour. I told her fifteen minutes would be fine. She told me that there would be "other, less well-known people on the bill." I didn't tell her that it would be pretty hard to find someone "less well-known" than I was! I suggested that Iván be included in the reading. My idea was that Iván could hear me and if he didn't like what he heard, he could skip the Larry Blake's reading, no hard feelings.

That fifteen-minute reading re-shaped my life. Iván loved what he heard and generously encouraged me. It was a pivotal moment. Here was a man whose own work was rich and powerful. I knew no one who even liked my work. At almost every point in my development, someone had told me *not* to do what I was doing. When I began to write multivoiced poems, a friend wrote me a letter urging me to *stop* writing them "They're terrible." When I showed another friend my long poems, she announced that long poems were boring. Iván gave me what I had never been able to find in all my years in the university system: validation, a sympathetic reading. The best poem I had produced at that point was "Turning Forty," a long collage piece initially influenced by David Bromige's "One Spring" but later by Joyce's *Finnegans Wake*. (I had often listened to Joyce's stunning recording of pages 213-216—the Anna Livia Plurabelle section.) For the reading at Larry Blake's I wrote a new poem in the style of "Turning Forty." It was called "Sweeney Adrift." Based on the ancient Irish poem, *Buille Suibhne,* it dealt freely with the legend of a mad Irish king. For the first (and last) time in my life I asked someone's opinion of my verse as I was actually composing it. I would write a few lines, phone Iván, read them to him, and he would say, "Great! Keep it coming!" I did. The opening lines of "Sweeney Adrift" carried a good deal of my literary history in it:

> welcome to the house of failure
> see these are the structural bases of the house its beams and
> arteries
> its artificial light its hands its vast appendices
> who is
> not here?
> the range of things
> delights us welcome welcome
>
> see there is the door it opens for us
> welcome

The reading at Larry Blake's (June 17, 1985) was a great success. It was attended by a few of my friends and many local poets—including Philip Lamantia and Nancy Peters—who wanted to hear Iván. Iván and I each went on to do many more readings, together or with others. Previously, if anyone was interested in my poetry, it was only because they were interested in me personally. For the first time, people were interested in me because they were interested in my poetry. "Sweeney Adrift" was much appreciated at Larry Blake's, as was "Overture: Chorus," the choral piece Adelle and I recited. No one had ever heard anything quite like it. Nancy Peters remarked to me that it was "original." Someone else told me that he was amazed at my performance because I seemed to be a "finished" poet, not a beginner, but no one had ever heard of me. I seemed, he said, to have come out of nowhere, as indeed I had! In all this, Adelle has been not only my wife but my performance partner. Her performing skills and her willingness to take the kinds of risks I ask of her have been enormous factors in my success. She has sung, tap-danced, made faces and screamed, all in the service of my "art." She has turned pieces which were at best only vaguely conceived into some sort of recognizable shape. People have said to me, "Well, *your* performance was all right, but *Adelle*...!" After a time of performing with me and listening to innumerable others, she began to write poetry herself, and her haiku appeared in various magazines. Her book, *Along the Bloodline*, has an introduction by me and blurbs from prominent local poets, including Michael McClure. After Adelle's death in 2016, I began to perform with my new love and performance partner, Sangye Land, who, as James

Broughton remarked, likewise helps me to inject a little more "multi" into my "cultural."

In 1986 I took over the series at Larry Blake's and then, in 1988, I was offered a radio show on KPFA, where I have been producing programs ever since. I became deeply involved with the community of writers here, organizing, discussing, reading, writing. From 1990 to 1995 I edited an Oakland-based magazine, *Poetry USA*. *Heaven Bone* called it "the poetry Bible of the 'Bay' area;" *The Beatlicks: Nashville's Poetry Newsletter* described its experimental issue as "a wake up call for poetry in America." In 1992 Joyce Jenkins named me contributing editor of her wonderful magazine, *Poetry Flash*. Larry Eigner, James Broughton, Al Young, Michael McClure, Jess, Ishmael Reed, and Lou Harrison became dear friends, and they have all encouraged my work in various ways. An appearance with Lou Harrison issued in a performance on his CD, *Lou Harrison: A Birthday Celebration*. On June 5, 2010, I received a Lifetime Achievement Award from The Berkeley Poetry Festival, and June 5, 2010 was "Jack Foley Day" in Berkeley. Adelle and I gave a performance and we had commemorative T shirts made. Later, I received a Lifetime Achievement Award from Marquis Who's Who.

There is much more to the story, but it will have to wait. If in the seventies I was completely unknown, in the past several years I have become an extremely public figure. "Sweeney Adrift" became a signature poem, and it was dedicated to Iván. "Chorus:

SON(G)," published like "Sweeney Adrift" in my book *Adrift*, is still another signature poem, and it is dedicated to someone I can only barely begin to discuss here: Jake Berry. Jake and I discovered each other's work in 1985 through a cassette magazine called *Poets 11*, and we have been encouraging and learning from each other ever since. He has been called, rightly, by Harry Polkinhorn, "the preeminent experimentalist of his generation." (Jake was born in 1959.) I wrote the preface to his *Brambu Drezi* and the afterword to his *Species of Abandoned Light*, both marvelous books. More recently, Neeli Cherkovski has joined our group. His lyricism and deep knowledge of poetic history are examples for us all. For some time now we have been nourishing one another, discussing poetry, acting like Something Is Afoot in California, thinking of ourselves as part of what John M. Bennett has called "the fundamental revolution going on in American poetry at this moment." Other energy sources include: Hank Lazer in Alabama, Bob Grumman in Florida, Susan Smith Nash in Oklahoma, Jim Leftwich in Virginia and Gregory Vincent St. Thomasino in New York. Writers recently designated as "The Other South" in *The New Orleans Review* connect with us as well. As Kenneth Rexroth, my predecessor at KPFA, wrote in "Disengagement: The Art of the Beat Generation" in 1957, "The avant-garde has not only not ceased to exist. It's jumping all over the place. Something's happening, man."

I should also mention here a kind of work that is at some distance from the passionate experimentalism I have been outlining.

That is the work of Dana Gioia and David Mason, leading lights of a movement called "The New Formalism." In the context of almost universal free verse, The New Formalism was perhaps another mode of experimentalism. In any case, I have never experienced the antipathy towards form that some experimentalists feel. I remember language poet David Melnick asking me, not out of curiosity but as a veiled attack, "Why do you *rhyme*?" In a sea of free versers, New Formalism was an affirmation of the continuing power of "traditional" verse. After all, so many of the poems I loved— including *all* of Yeats—were in traditional verse. Dana and I have become close friends and admirers of each other's work. I wrote this about him:

> The secret of Dana Gioia's formalism is not the desire to bring back something outmoded, done—though the dead are a heavy presence in his work—but the desire to make something *beautiful*, and to make it in a way that is recognizable, in a way that others may share. It seems an old-fashioned enterprise to be looking for beauty—something out of the 19th century—yet it is precisely a sense of beauty that is missing from so much current work. What beauty—not what puzzle, not what ironic stance, not what deconstruction, not what politics, not what language-oriented consciousness, not what poetics—is possible for *us*, writers *post* so much we can scarcely discover to what we are *pre*? Gioia's angel, though as defaced as Rilke's Apollo, has at least one wing left to bring us into the presence of what was once considered holy.

Composer/poet Lou Harrison—whose own verse was syllabic—said to me once, emphatically, "*We* (California artists) *are not frightened of beauty!*"

In 2018 Dana Gioia and Peter Whitfield published *Jack Foley's Unmanageable Masterpiece*, a book dealing with my *Visions and Affiliations*, a two-volume, 1300-page "chronoencyclopedia" of California poetry stretching from 1940 to 2005. Published in 2011 by Iván Argüelles's Pantograph Press, *Visions and Affiliations* had been hailed by critic Marjorie Perloff as "overwhelming! What a great time line and fabulous encyclopedia. I really am learning so much. A great read and great information. I don't know how you did it. Your enthusiasm and first-hand knowledge show on every page." Gioia and Whitfield write, "In 2011 a tiny press in Berkeley published *Visions and Affiliations*, an eccentric 1300-page chronology of post-war California literature in two massive paperbound folio volumes. With no commercial distribution or publicity, the book sold about two hundred copies and soon vanished from sight—but not from the memory of the small audience that read it. Some of them considered the elaborate time line the first adequate account of California's complex and contradictory literary life. Others recognized Foley's radical innovation in changing how literary history could be written. A few even considered the strange, sprawling, yet compulsively readable tomes an oddball masterpiece."

Visions and Affiliations arose out of certain speculations made in my earlier books, *O Powerful Western Star* and *Foley's Books*—a pair of books published in 2000 in which I collected a wide variety of essays and reviews I had written for *Poetry Flash* and for *The Alsop Review*. *O Powerful Western Star* even contained a CD in which Adelle and I performed some of the work in the book as well as one of my most successful choruses: "CHORUS: SON(G)." I believe the CD is one of the few—if not the only—instance of criticism as a performance art. Influenced deeply by Walter J. Ong, the book also contains a statement about performance poetry. I delivered it as part of "The Performance Poetry Bash" at Fort Mason, San Francisco, for Herman Berlandt's National Poetry Week II (San Francisco, 1988):

> Camerado, this is no book...
>   —Walt Whitman, "So Long"

> Performance poetry is an active and intellectually engaged response to the silence and whiteness in which most poetry remains entangled. Writing of Mallarmé, Frederick R. Karl remarked, "The page or territory is primary, on which language wanders like a lonely adventurer hoping to survive emptiness and whiteness." The performance poet insists that s/he is not a mere adjunct of a book but rather a manifestation of what books arise out of: the physical presence of the author. Historically, "poetry" and "writing" remain in a state of tension. (Homer was a poet, not a writer.) Performance poetry seeks to tilt that tension in the direction of presence, to insist on the limitations of writing as a medium for the presentation of the art. At the heart of

writing, at the heart of all mass culture, is a profound and disturbing absence. Performance poetry is an insistence that absence, silence and whiteness—the page—are not the only conditions in which poetry can be "heard."

I have been writing about my learning years. How often the words "Berkeley" and "KPFA" appear in this account. In an ecstatic moment of his poem, *Poet in New York*, Federico Garcia Lorca, looking about him in Harlem, cries out, "Negroes! Negroes! Negroes!" I might equally have cried out, "Berkeley! Berkeley! Berkeley!" I had come to California to be educated by the University of California at Berkeley. That education, while it lasted, gave me some things of value but, all in all, it did not quite take. The *city* of Berkeley, however, with all of its cultural opportunities, its openness to the arts, its support of listener-sponsored KPFA, its nearness to both San Francisco and Oakland—very different literary/cultural centers—all this gave me the education I wished to find. Books and the Bay Area were more my university than the university I attended. In a city of contrarians, I was deeply at home. Where else could one receive the education one received from the FSM? Where else could one find someone writing with great compassion and empathy about the Ohlone? Where else could one find bookstores like Moe's and Cody's and Black Oak, among others? Heidegger describes *Dasein* as "thrown" into the world; over fifty years ago, I was thrown into the Bezerkely world of Berkeley, and it was Berkeley that opened me to so much. What I discovered there was the self-consciousness of a city that attempted to rewrite history in every way. *Why couldn't we make the world better? Why couldn't we change things?* I mentioned that on June 5, 2010, I was deeply honored to receive a Lifetime Achievement Award from The Berkeley Poetry Festival; as part of the festivities, that day was named "Jack Foley Day." Adelle was by my side as we gave a poetry reading as part of the event. And in August, 2019, a plaque awarded to me by Marquis Who's Who was hung on the wall at KPFA. This was better than a PhD, honorary or otherwise. The very place that had furnished me with so much acknowledged me as a portion of its own cultural heritage. Very little of my education had to do specifically with "institutions of higher learning," though I attended some and it was important that Berkeley was a university town. But it was *Dasein*—"being there," in Berkeley, in "laid-back," culturally electric California—that made it all happen. Where but in Oz can such transformative experiences be found?

*

THE DIFFICULTY OF CONCLUDING THIS AUTOBIOGRAPHY

What you either come by naturally, or as I suspect have always understood is how to free your mind.

—Barbara Guest in a letter to me

...

I offer you this mantra—the fruit of so much of twentieth-century thought: *some parts of the mind don't know what other parts of the mind are doing.*

—Jack Foley

Looking back over this short autobiography, I realize how much of my life I've been *un*able to name in it. Even what I have been able to name is problematical. In story our lives tend to take on a coherence and purpose which they may well have lacked in actuality. As circumstances arise we discover/invent "selves" to deal with them. And the circumstances change in response to those selves. What I wrote in the 70's in a paper on Alfred Hitchcock ("Doubleness in Hitchcock: Seeing the Family Plot") might apply more generally—not merely in the Oedipal sense—to my understanding of the world: "In the dizzying ramifications of the Oedipal situation the external world and the self are not separate entities but dynamic forces which shift, merge, interrelate, conflict, reverberate, change around—and the very same narcissistic tendencies which give rise to (among other things) fantasies of murder become, in the limitations and intensities of 'performance,' a mode of authentic self-disclosure. In the midst of a self-reflective world, a world in which actor and audience tend to merge, and which tends to give back, reflect the ramifications of the self, 'action' becomes in effect *revelatory*."

"Performance," "action," and the "revelatory" have been key factors in my work. Hannah Arendt's chapter on "Action" in *The Human Condition* quotes Dante: "For in every action what is primarily intended by the doer, whether he acts from natural necessity or out of free will, is the disclosure of his own image. Hence it comes about that every doer, in so far as he does, takes delight in doing; since everything that is desires its own being, and since in action the being of the doer is somehow intensified, delight necessarily follows...Thus, nothing acts unless [by acting] it makes patent its latent self."

One might also cite Baudelaire, whose sonnet, "Correspondences," I recently translated. (I added a quotation from Swedenborg to Baudelaire's poem to show Baudelaire's own source of the word "correspondence.")

> What correspondence is is not known at the present day, for several reasons, the chief of which is that man has withdrawn himself from heaven by the love of self and love

of the world...This was not so with the ancient people. To them the knowledge of correspondences was the chief of knowledges. By means of it they acquired intelligence and wisdom; and by means of it those who were of the church had communication with heaven; for the knowledge of correspondences is angelic knowledge. The most ancient people, who were celestial men, thought from correspondence itself, as the angels do. Therefore they talked with angels, and frequently saw the Lord and were taught by Him. But at this day that knowledge has been so completely lost that no one knows what correspondence is.

Emanuel Swedenborg, *Heaven and Its Wonders
and Hell* (1758)

Nature is a temple where living statues
At times give out confused words;
Man passes through forests of symbols
That watch him with familiar looks.

Like long echoes that merge from afar
In a shadowy and profound unity,
Vast like the night, like light,
Perfumes, colors and sounds answer back and forth.

There are perfumes as fresh as the flesh of infants,
Soft, like oboes, green, like fields,
—And others, corrupt, rich and triumphant,
Having the expansion of infinite things .

Amber, musk, benzoin, incense,
Singing the **transports** of spirit and sense.

Poetry does not arise out of a *part* of one's life. It permeates everything, welcomes everything. When Iván was just beginning to write his great epic poem, *Pantograph*, he phoned me to talk about it. *"No more inhibitions!"* he said triumphantly. I thought of that remark when I wrote the following lines in "Villanelle," a poem dedicated to Iván:

> THE DESCENT INTO HELL & DARKNESS & THE NEED FOR "MEHR LICHT" are primal images, gestures. Song allows us to contemplate horrors & yet remain sane. It places the horrific thing directly in front of us, we see it all, & clearly, yet, because of the song, it *cannot* harm us. Song empties the terrible of its terror, annihilates *content*, yet leaves us with a "sweetness" that is certainly close to if it is not precisely a state of grace, a Buddhistic emptiness. Song seems to distance us from the world at the same time that it brings the world to us, with all its "news." Song's "sweetness" allows us a certain innocence in the midst of the inferno. Shhhhh, it says to the horrors, there's nothing going on here, only someone humming a tune.

I remember as well the title of Larry Eigner's first mature book: *From the Sustaining Air*. The "airs" a poet puts on sustain him in innumerable ways. These are some lines from a recent piece; the concluding word is meant as a pun:

> The drowned day
> any man of vigorous mind
> anticipate his thought
> which all ranks pay
> I cannot even hear of Vigor of any kind
> bread and fire
> I know not
> *lyre*

I believe the thrust of so much current writing involves a redefinition of selfhood. The remarks Ludwig Wittgenstein makes about the concept of "games" in *Philosophical Investigations* might be a description of the kind of "self" we see in some current work. Wittgenstein is attempting to define "games," to find some "essence" that is common to all of them—and he is unable to do that: "If you look at [games] you will not see something that is common to *all*, but similarities, relationships, and a whole series of them at that...And we extend our concept...as in spinning a thread we twist fibre on fibre. *And the strength of the thread does not reside in the fact that some one fibre runs through the whole length, but in the overlapping of many fibres*" (my italics).

In a little paper on "Hamlet's 'Individuality'" I argued that the supposed "individuality" of Shakespeare's character was in fact "multiplicity." One might say the same thing of the figure which emerges from autobiography:

The fact is that Hamlet seems real not because he is a coherent character or "self" or because there is some discoverable "essence" to him but because *he actively and amazingly inhabits so many diverse, interconnecting, potentially contradictory contexts.* Implicitly promising to tell us all about the interesting "individual" Hamlet, the *play Hamlet* ends by expressing the possibility that "individuality" (a word derived from the Latin *individuus*, indivisible) *is in fact multiplicity.* It is the plenitude of contexts in which Hamlet functions—i.e., his multiplicity—that gives him density.

*

We're supposed to be these unities. *And we're not.*
    —Jess, in conversation

I was born.

    Jack Foley
    4/13/96
    (revised 11/2020)

When I began this project, I asked a few people who were close to me to write a few sentences about me. I told them I would not edit what they wrote or respond to it in any way. I also told them that it didn't have to be positive.

Jack's life, like his art, is based in collage. He welcomes unorthodox combinations of everything from food to music, from friends to clothing—and urges them enthusiastically on those around him. Living with Jack is a lifelong, year-round course of study with no boundaries and no written exams.

    Like nobody else
    His passions stretch and challenge
    What "everyone knows"

        Adelle Foley
        4/26/96

Courage and faith are the two words that come to mind when I think about my father. This may be an odd thing to say about an ex-Catholic, but I don't think I have met a person who is more willing to challenge the assumptions of everyone around him and confident enough to forge his own path. There are four examples in my father's life that illustrate this point: his friendship with Larry Eigner, his poetry, his decision to drop out of graduate school and his kindness to those around him.

Sean Foley
4/27/96

FIVE THINGS ABOUT JACK FOLEY

Jack-
If you can read it I can write it
                M

1. Jack Foley is one of the main hombres for shouldering responsibilities in the Bay Area literary world; whether it's friendship and care-giving for cerebral-palsied poet friends or letting everyone know about an important event that might be missed, Jack is there with his shoulder to the wheel and his hand on the phone.

2. Jack is notable for the specialness of his ear and he's capable of, and likely to, appreciate the most far-flung temperaments from experimental Jake Berry to gay and metaphysical James Broughton.

3. It's as if Jack runs an ever-open service to stick up for the rights of the outcast and the unaligned or invalided writers. He reminds others of their responsibility through his activism.

4. Jack never forgets a birthday whether it's his own or yours. He's right there to celebrate.

5. In roles like public radio reviewer-maestro-and contributing editor to *Poetry Flash*, Jack is a deepener; he has a powerful intellect and gives substance to issues under view.

Michael McClure
4/12/96
(Automatic Writing)

It was reported in the Oakland Daily Tribulation that someone had broken into the First Rational Bank and had made off with quantities of ballpoint pens. Rumors that Jack Foley is the culprit are irresponsible and inaccurate. I was with Jack and Adelle from the beginning of his memorable poetry reading to the wee hours of the morning. Who could forget the guitar-dancing, tap-twanging multisimultaneous poetic cavortings. It was entertaining and affecting. Afterwards we repaired to their house and, surrounded by treasures and artifacts that attest to the Foley passion for the arts, we talked of all shapes of cabbages and all sorts of kings. Jack's breadth of knowledge and depth of insight are impressive. There was laughter too, much nose-clearing, eye-opening, twittering-tittering. Early on it was all poetry and performance, exciting new sounds, voices, ideas and deeply human caring. Later it was sharing and clashing, some sanity and much insanity at the Foley home...a full and remarkable night. So Jack Foley could not have robbed the bank...unless he had an accomplice.

Artist Leonard Breger
4/96

Jack's all right if you like that kind of person.

> The D D D Monster
> 4/96

EEEEE. EEEEEE. EEEEEEEEEE. EEEEEE. E.
> The E E E Monster
> 4/96

ADDENDUM

ADELLE'S DEATH (2016)

I went through Adelle's death with her as she finally succumbed to stomach cancer. That sad event now belongs to this story. It was horrible to see her suffer, though there were moments of tenderness and love. I would have done anything to save her. I would have given my life for hers. But there was nothing I could do. Neither of us believed in life after death. I wanted to die when she died, but life finally wins in the end—partially. At any rate, life continues. I didn't die and, to my surprise, I found that I could love again. I survived the death she had to die. But no matter how much laughter and love I still retained within me, I became a man of sorrow, touched by the stain of death.

FROM **GRIEF SONGS (2017)**

From *RIVERRUN* (in *scriptio continua*):

asweagewediscovertoourdismaythatrelationshipswehadexp
ectedtolastalifetimedisappear:l
ovedones,eventhemarvelousones,die.inanageofskepticism,i
nwhichtheheavenstoriescarrylittleweight,howdo
wedealwiththisimmenselydisturbingsituation,thisblowtoallo
uregotism?

*

I told Adelle, through tears, that I wished with all my heart
that the news had been given to me. She said
she would have felt the same way.
            —June 5, 2016

Perhaps it's best to begin with Dellwackia. For many years, Adelle and I drew cartoons for each other. We were the only people who saw them. The central figures were a king, Jack Wack (me— "J.W.") and a queen, Dell Dell (a name Adelle's father used to call her), but there were many others including Jack Wack and Dell Dell Dog; Young Lioness and her mate; Salvador Dully (the tiny sun— not small because he was distant but small because he was small); Looney (the moon); Iacchus Wacchus, the Roman, with his mate, Della Della Puella Bella; Dr. Quack with his nurse, Flowence Nightindell (whenever anyone falls ill, Dr. Quack is sent on an all-expenses-paid trip to someplace else: everyone likes him, but no one wants him tending the sick—though no one really gets sick in Dellwackia); etc.

They inhabited a country named for the queen and king: Dellwackia. Everything—rocks, trees, everything—in Dellwackia talked. The figures had voices which Adelle and I provided, and they became an everyday fixture of our life. There was never a day in which, at various times, we didn't speak in the voices to one another. When I told Adelle I had an appointment with the podiatrist, she immediately said, "Jack Wack Dog needs to have his toenails clipped!" Jack Wack and Dell Dell were comic, parodic, child-like, but they were also possessed of the pure love that children manifest: "Daddy!" "Mommy!" If sometimes something went wrong with Jack and Adelle, nothing ever went wrong with them. They believed in what they called, "LLLLAAAAAHHHHVVVEEE." And we could become them whenever we wished.

When, in her last days, Adelle apologized to me for being "grumpy"—which she wasn't, she was brave and loving and intelligent—she did so in the voice of Dell Dell. (Like some children, Dellwackians pronounced their r's as w's, though there was one instance in which they pronounced a w as an r: the famous pulp fiction character, The Shadow became in Dellwackia "The ShadoR." As a Dellwackian, of course, he didn't "know" very much. He regularly forgot to put eye holes in his mask so that, though he could be seen, he couldn't see anyone else.)

It depressed me enormously to think that that whole world we had created would simply vanish with Adelle's death, so I took a look at the cartoons we had saved. I was surprised to find that they were better than I thought: some of them had enormous energy. (At one point we were doing them every day.) It occurred to me that they might even be made public. At least that way they would have some staying power. I should add that they were begun and worked on long before I had any fame as a poet—I was nothing more than a graduate student at UC Berkeley—and, again, they were originally meant for no one's eyes but Adelle's and mine.

Wednesday, June 15, 2016, 12 days before her death, 10 days before her lapsing into a coma from which she never awoke, Adelle wrote in the voice of her cartoon character, Dell Dell:

> "SOWWY
> Nous toutes don't mean to be gwumpy.
> We LLLLAAAHHHVVVEEESSS
> tous les gars
> Who are generous and loving and v stwessed."

Later, on the phone, she asked me whether I forgave her: "Does forgive?" Yes.

["Nous toutes"—"all of us" (female)—and "tous les gars"—"all the guys"—are references to a song by Georges Brassens, a song Adelle and I both loved: "Brave Margot." Brave Adelle!]

On June 16, Father's Day, Adelle felt sad that she hadn't gotten anything for me. Though I knew she had a significant tremor in her writing hand, I asked her to make me a cartoon. She did. There are lines that betray the presence of the tremor, but the figure comes through loud and clear: Dell Dell is saying, "love, love, love."

...

My dear wife Adelle was diagnosed with cancer on Saturday, June 4, 2016. She was intelligent and brave and loving throughout the struggle. I told her doctor, "We want to keep her." Adelle chimed in, "I want to be kept." In 1960—we were both twenty—she had sung an ancient French song, "A la Claire

Fontaine," to me. It was a sweet gesture of young love. The refrain of the song is "Il y a longtemps que je t'aime / Jamais je ne t'oublierai" ("I have loved you for a long time / I will never forget you"). Over the years we often sang the song together. In 2016 I sang the song to her as she lay dying in the hospital: "I have loved you for a long time / I will never forget you." She died June 27, 2016. I wrote many years ago:

> It's not a dream
> We lose those we love
> > but we love
> > > anyway

*

MY WIFE ADELLE'S DEATH

What you discover in such a situation
is what Rousseau called
le néant des choses humaines
the nothingness of human affairs
Adelle's concerns—the laundry, our finances,
her plants, dinner, people at AC Transit, people
in the local community, poetry people, whether
I parked the car close enough to the curb,
her VISA card, the Toyota, her haiku, the goldfish, me,
the light in the leaves as she passed by in the morning,
credit cards, J.R.R. Tolkien, Octavia Butler, *Miss Fisher's Murder Mysteries*, the egrets at Lake Merritt,
the homeless on her way to AC Transit
(to whom she gave money and boxes of raisins),
her son and daughter in law,

hundreds of others
in a complex web of caring—
all disappeared poof in a few moments
on the afternoon of June 25, 2016
in a Kaiser hospital room
when she fainted in "septic shock" and her dear heart
stopped.
Suddenly, all of that was gone
as if it never existed
le néant des choses humaines
I remember it, some of it—even most of it—but for her
it's a spider web someone brushed off a window—
gone.
It is this that we make poems and stories and beautiful lies
to avoid:
this sudden view
when a long-loved, long-known, long-accepted person dies
& we see it
deep and clear

...

FOR MAW SHEIN WIN, WHO LOST HER SISTER

How do you come back to life
When someone close to you
Someone who is you—
A wife, a sister—
Is suddenly gone.
"Don't forget to bring the dearth certificate,"
A friend accidentally wrote:
He called it, accurately, a dearth, an absence, a loss
But it is more than that:
It is a diminution
That draws us into its darkness.

The struggle of the other's dearth
Is also the knowledge of our own
Our own diminishment
Until we wish to be the
Nothing
Our loved one has become: smoke, vapor.
When my wife died,
I walked through my kitchen
Weeping
And saying, "I want to die."
I know she would have never wished that for me
And yet
The strength of death—its lure—
Was that strong.
Our love, our happy life together
Brought to a sudden end—
My wife, your sister.
Why do ghosts
Rattle chains and frighten strangers?
Let them return
To where they will be loved and appreciated.
Let them live in our hearts.
Look: the house still has your scent in it;
Your clothing hangs in the closet!
Dear Maw,
Let us both
Try to bear the unbearable,
Try to live
In a world which has taken the dearest thing to us
And destroyed it, though we knew
From the beginning that that was possible,
That death was the price of life.
But we know it now
In a way that is different from what we knew.

SANGYE

I think grief might be defined as the simultaneous absence and presence of the loved one. To some extent we feel this with anyone who is not around, but the stunning fact of death intensifies the feeling beyond belief. We don't "get over" grief: we subsume it, it becomes a part of us. Death as a life-changing event! I felt that Adelle's death turned me—no matter how much joy and laughter I have left—into a man of sorrow. That, I think, is really what Coleridge's "Ancient Mariner" is about. The "moral" at the end— "He prayeth best who loveth best"—is just icing on the cake for 19th-century readers. It's really about the stain of death.

I met Sangye Land, daughter of poet Julie Rogers, stepdaughter of poet David Meltzer, on December 28, 2016. I came to the house Sangye and Julie shared with David to pay my respects to my old friend, who was on his deathbed. I wanted to say goodbye and to tell him what I would say about him after his death—which I did. The full weight of grief was still upon me and I appeared with that dark shadow hanging over me. I hardly expected to fall in love, but that is what happened. I had seen Sangye once before—at a distance—and thought her astonishingly beautiful. Today, her mother was grieving and less visible, and Sangye, though grieving also, was greeting visitors and escorting them in to see David. I had come to the house with my friend Carl Landauer, and there were several people there. As I entered, Sangye walked over to me, hand extended, and said, "I don't believe I know you." I was stunned.

What do you say when a beautiful woman indicates that she would like to know you? You tell her about yourself, you ask about her. As I waited, and as she rose to greet people, Sangye and I spoke. I don't remember exactly what we said—though I recall something about Yeats (I was surprised to discover that she hadn't read him), about her interest in the Irish, about a poem of David's that was a mutual favorite ("I love that poem!" she said), and about Italians who pinch. But the words were all like music accompanying a scene that goes beyond words. I was certainly falling in love but the situation seemed utterly impossible: she was far too young. I was not even very clear about her name, which I had never heard before. It was some time later, through Facebook, that I discovered how to spell it. (It means "Buddha" in Tibetan: like some of my heroes—Allen Ginsberg, for example—she is Tibetan Buddhist.)

As I drove home with Carl I could do nothing but talk about the lovely young woman I had met. Love had seemed dead in me, yet here it was springing up again—near Christmas, no less. I immediately wrote the poem which follows, but I had no idea how I could send it to her. It didn't seem like a good idea to send it to her mother. Its title was taken from the title of a collection by Antonin Artaud:

50 DESIGNS TO MURDER MAGIC

Can you say she took your breath away
Yes, I can say that
But you talked on to her

And that
        Required
                Breath
Can you say
She was beautiful
Yes, I can say that
        Her hair especially was beautiful
                And her serious
                        Eyes
        But she was also
                Exceptionally kind
She listened when you spoke
        Yes, and laughed
                When I said
                        Something amusing
Yet her laughter seemed almost
        Reluctant
        As if she couldn't quite help herself
As if something came from within
(As something came from within me)

There was no way on earth we could be lovers

As I left she said, "It was wonderful to meet you"
I thanked her for being so considerate

                        Her hair moved often
                        As she moved

As it turned out, it wasn't at all necessary to murder magic.
Our first date—magic again—was on Valentine's Day, 2017. Soon,
Sangye and I began to live together, and we began to imagine a new
life in which it was possible for an old death-haunted man and a
young woman to love each other and to respond to the very different

needs each of them might manifest at any time. I wrote this for one
of her birthdays:

> There is a long lake
> And trees surrounding it
> In a womb-like formation
> With marvelous, shifting
> Clouds in the deep blue sky.
> I know this lake
> Doesn't exist
> But I think of it
> As where you were born
> In Oregon
> A womb place
> To which your mind returns
> And to which, now,
> My mind has access.
> I think of you
> Emerging from it
> With the magical name
> Sangye
> Defining you.
> There are birds
> In this forest
> But they are silent
> As your consciousness
> Arises
> And comes into the world.
> None of this is real.
> It is story
> Something I made up
> To fill my mind
> With what I cannot
> Know:
> Your origin.
> Were there wings

That you discarded
At the lake
And a quiet, bearded boatman
To deliver you to this world?
Was there another you
Before this one?
What was your history?
What was the little girl
Who looked around her
At a world
Which at times
Would be cruel to her?
What lies were you told?
What truths?
What is it that makes you
Sometimes shudder?
Is it the memory
Of that lake, that forest
Those marvelous,
Abandoned
Wings?
Did the boatman betray you?
None of this is true
And yet truth enters into it
And a magic world
That radiates
Delight and fear and love.
What were they, those clouds,
Those trees, that lake, those wings diaphanous?
Could they protect
The living soul
That arose in magic
And carried with it
Traces
Of that Nowhere,
That magic Land
Through all your loved, tumultuous, passionate, fiery days.

And this for her on one of my birthdays:

> you are as always the angel of my heart
> the one whose wings guard me from the dark
> one whose love encircles the deepening space
> that we inhabit as we spin through the wide, wide range of
> our lives
> lives that have mixed love with grief, success with failure,
> despair with hope (*désespoir/espoir*), sobbing with laughter
> and all in a dark time in which the vile
> rise up and claim the goodness of earth
> you are the angel the one who holds me to my better selves
> and speaks love and hope to my eager, listening ears

In 2018 Sangye wrote this gorgeous, loving poem to me:

Just Some Of The Reasons Why I Love You -
From A - Z

A is because you're Adorable, Affectionate, Authentic and
the Apple of my eye.
B is for all the Books you've written and your deep,
abiding love for the written word.
C is because you're Captivating and you Care for me.
D is for your Depth, your Daring Do, your Delicious lips,
and Decadent kisses.
E is for your Enthusiasm and your Empathy.
F is for your Fertile mind, Fearless stage performances, and
Fantastically skilled Fingers.
G is for your Goodness, your Generosity, your Gorgeous
eyes, Gregarious personality, and because I'm so Glad I
met you.
H is for your Heart. 💜
I hold it in my Heart. 💜

I is for your Intellect and your myriad Interests.

J is for your Jack Talk - need I say more?

K is for your Kisses (I just can't get enough), your Keenness and your Kindness.

L is for the Love we share.

M is for your Mischievous streak, your Motivation and because thankfully, you're Mine.

N is because you're a Natty dresser, you give great Nookie, you're Noteworthy and you Nourish Me.

O is for your Observant nature, your Optimism, your Openness, and because you're an Original.

P is for your Passion, your Playfulness, your Poetry, and because you're Precious and dare I say, Priceless to me.

Q is because you're Quick-Witted, Quirky and you've become Quintessential to my happiness.

R is for your Romantic nature and your Rarity.

S is for your Smile and because you're Sexy, Sensitive, and Sweet.

T is because I suspected that I was in Trouble the day I met you, I was Terrified to fall in love with you and you show me how Terrific you are each and every day.

U is because you're Unusual in the best possible sense of the word.

V is because you're my one and only Valentine and I love you Very, Very much.

W is because you're Wonderful and I Wished for you before I knew you existed.

X is for all our X rated moments - how I love them!

Y is for Your art, Your Musicality, and Your Rhythm. Y is for You - my Baby.

Z is because you're Zippy, Zingy, and Zealous.

I'm not a poet (as far as I know) but I do love you, Honey.

Happy Father's Day.

*

FINALE 2020

It is a terrific problem that faces the poet today—a world that is so in transition from a decayed culture toward a reorganization of human evaluations that there are few common terms, general denominators of speech that are solid enough or that ring with any vibration or spiritual conviction.

...

Did I tell you of that thrilling experience this last winter In the dentist's chair when under the influence of aether and amnesia my mind spiraled to a kind of seventh heaven of consciousness and egoistic dance among the seven spheres—and something like an objective voice kept saying to me—"You have the higher consciousness—you have the higher consciousness. This is something that very few have. This is what is called genius."? A happiness, ecstatic such as I have known only twice in "inspirations" came over me. I felt the two worlds. And at once. As the bore went into my tooth I was able to follow Its every revolution as detached as a spectator at a funeral. O Gorham, I have known moments in eternity.

—Hart Crane

We live in a history of "the new."

—Jack Foley

Recently I have begun to think of Modernism as the search for a language—a language in which it would be possible to express that Modernist word, the "new," a "transition from a decayed culture toward a reorganization of human evaluations." I would include movements such as Dada and Futurism, texts such as Pound's *Cantos*, Eliot's *Waste Land*, Vallejo's *Trilce*, Joyce's attacks on the English language in *Finnegans Wake*, Stein's *Tender Buttons*, Yeats' attempt to create a sacred, "occult" language of poetry in *The Wind Among the Reeds*, Hart Crane's work, influenced by Ouspensky, Heidegger's restructuring of German in *Sein und Zeit*, Mayakovsky, Artaud's wild cries in his "radiodiffusion," *Pour En Finir Avec Le Jugement De Dieu*, Wittgenstein's speculations, Zukofsky's homophonic translations of Catullus, many others. More recent work might be included as well: Iván Argüelles' wild, erudite, simultaneously Surrealist, Classical, and South Asian mentations, Jake Berry's *Brambu Drezi*, John M. Bennett's visual-literary work, excursions into the asemic, again many others. Some of my own wilder pieces, such as this attempt in *scriptio continua*, come out of this desire as well, I think:

AIRPLANESZOOMINGFROMOAKLANDTONOWHEREFRO
MOAKLANDTOEVERYWHEREFROMNORTHERNCALIFTO
THEDEEPDEEPSOUTHFRIENDSSIGHINGANDFRYINGINTH
EHEATINTHESKILLETSINTHE*LARRUPIN*'SOUTH
LANGUAGE/SOUNDPLACESACONTEXTABURDENOFMEA
NINGUPONUSTHEMOMENTTHESPEAKEROF*THEWAKE*BE
GINSTOTALK("the night was clear though i slept i seen
It")HISWORLDAWAKENSAWALKERINHISWORLDTHETON
GUETHELINGUATHEOLDPALAVERTHEFIRE("none will loc
but the wind will cum")"THEWAECEND"

HOTSEPTEMBERDAYSGIVINGMENEWSOFLIMITATIONSL
APSESOFENERGYINTHEHEATLOVEFORTHEHOUSEFAN
IWRITEANDDOWHATICAN.ITINTERESTSME,KEEPSMEALI
VE.BUTIHAVENOREASONTOBELIEVETHATAFTERMYDE
ATHANYONEWILLCAREABOUTMYWRITING.IT'SEXTRE
MELYDIFFICULTTOKNOWWHATWRITINGWILLLASTAND
WHATWILLNOTBUTIHAVE*NO*INDICATIONSTHATMINEWI
LLLAST.MYENTHUSIASMSHAVEBEENINTENSEANDIHAV
ETRIEDTOEMBODYTHEM—EMBODYWHAT*ITHINK*—
BUTTHEREAREVERYFEWPEOPLEWHOADMIREMYWORK
ANDIBELIEVEI*KNOW*THEMALL!THISDOESNOTINDICATE
THEPOSSIBILITYOFLASTINGFAMEORINFLUENCE.I'MALL
RIGHTWITHTHIS:IT'SJUSTTHEWAYTHINGSARE.IDIDMYB
EST.

THEBATWASISOLATEDINTHELIVINGROOM.THEYHANG
ONDRAPESWHENTHEYDON'TMOVESOTHEYAREN'TALL
THATHARDTOLOCATE.IHADCLOSEDTHEGLASSDOORS.T
HEFRONTDOORWASOPEN.THEBATWASMOTIONLESSON
THELIVINGROOMRUG.ICAREFULLYWENTROUNDTOTHE
FRONTROOMTOCLOSETHEDOORSOITCOULDN'TGETBAC
KTHERE.I*MAY*HAVESEENITJUSTASITEXITEDTHEFRONTD
OOR.THEYLOOKLIKESHADOWSWHENTHEYFLYBY.

This language is not achieved but continually attempted, continually indicated as possible. I recently thought of the attempt

to achieve it as the sounds coming from the severed head of
Orpheus:

ORPHÉE

"Do you speak French?"
—Suzanne Verdal

c'est la tête qui chante
après la mort
après la grande Perte
c'était le projet
du Modernisme
de chercher une langue
nouvelle

une langue
qui chante
après la mort

une langue
sans histoire
comme la langue
des oiseaux

je suis le poète
de cette langue

impossible

la tête d'orphée
qui chante avec une force très grande

comme un aveugle
qui tape à la machine

Perhaps that will be my epitaph: comme un aveugle / qui tape à la machine.

Michael McClure on Jack Foley (2012):

BEGINNING WITH LINES BY THE POET

for JACK FOLEY

"THIS MAN LOOKS OUT AT ME
eyes full of interest and perhaps suffering
whatever he looks at registered on his face…"
Just that much and not more would be enough,
always though he is dancing like his dad, shuffling
canny strange steps of thirties and 3000 a.d.
KNOWLEDGE OF POETRY
Finds him and Adelle
opening Clyfford Still's mystery:
Let figure and ground fuse into one.
Eyes tell a little more than the ear hears.
Yes, his poetry breathes intelligence

BUT
it's also aloft with intuition.
He recreated the Batman Gallery
but did not ever touch his winged
feet on those Fillmore Street boards.
Bards welcomed him there and then,
and inspired artists painted his
IMAGINATION.
He goes on to triumph through the modes:
from archetypal Olsonian projectivity
of post-heroic deconstruction
to eructation of naughty nursery rhymes
without a solecism in sight.

Like Cocteau, "Radio Daddy"
made tubes and circuits sing Poetry
in voices of Whitman and Gertrude Stein
(and, almost, Emily Dickinson).

He
oped
airways
multiculturally,
and with catholicity
speaks the finest and sees
the highest possible
in other.
IN CREATING THE INEFFABLE
POETRY TIME LINE OF CALIFORNIA
he presented it as most effable,
and in the loop and trajectory
of the unknown, but now known,
history of the work he became
at one with
the work. (The *POEIN)*

—Did Goethe create Faust
or vice versa?—

Loving all poesy from L=A=N=G=U=A=G=E
to dangling American foot
he uncovered the root
of unpremeditated wit
AND IN THE PASTURES
flowered by their strophes,
he sings forth with his better
half,
THE LADY
A
D
E
L
L
E
:

Shepherd and shepherdess of vocable
and volta
with joyful tongue
and breeze-stroked lyra.

"Thus are things decreed by fate.
Esti gar eimarmena pantos…"

*Manannan mac Lir
(Michael McClure)*

Jack Foley on Michael McClure (2020):

THE KING, THE PRINCE, THE POET

for Michael McClure (October 20, 1932-May 4, 2020)

The prince is dead.
Defender of whales.
It didn't seem possible.
The great one
Who read his work at
The most famous of all
San Francisco readings
Six Gallery, 1955.
The one who voiced his poems
To the marvelous melodies
Of Ray Manzarek,
From whom Janis Joplin
Stole a song,
The one who told me,
"People who wear black

Are in mourning for themselves."
The king is dead.
The one who survived
Everything
And lived to sing of it,
The one who spoke
Chaucer in the original
So that people might know
Where our language came from.
The king, the prince, the poet
Who rose from Wichita
And embodied San Francisco
Who called to the birds near his home
Who answered.
"We were making," he told me,
"The myth of ourselves."
He survived so much
It seemed likely
That Death would make an exception
In his case
(No, he did not have Coronavirus!)
But this wonderful man
Is gone from us.
His Angel weeps.
Her name is Amy
And she will forever be
His love, his partner
Though there was another
Who loved him too.
Dear Angel, whose wings
Will have to fly in a different way
To find him now.
I loved them both
And learned from them.
She survives to build a world
Around herself in which
Michael forever is

And isn't
While she goes on.
May she fly, as she always has,
With sweet, compassionate dignity.
May her delicate hands
Build figures (embodiments) that live forever
As Michael's words
Will live forever.
There is a world
That does not die.
The Muses
Weep.

.

ELEGY

The animals are clamoring
The deer
The hawks circling
The squirrels
All the inhabitants of the zoo
The lions in the San Francisco Zoo
They are all making noises
The monkeys howl
Dogs and cats in the streets
The incredible coyotes
Strolling in the city
The fish
The whales
Even the tiny things, the ants, the bugs, mosquitos
Everything
Even the living trees
That bend to the wind
Near the water
The ocean the sand
The monkeys

They are all muttering or crying
Or howling outright
And the animals that are people
The "mammal nation"—
All these creatures know
They clamor they "complain" (in the old sense)
That the poet McClure is gone
Though they cannot
       tell you where

JACK FOLEY ON THE INTERNET

Audio

JACK & ADELLE FOLEY: PERFORMANCES

"Words & Books, Poetry & Writing;" "Chorus: SON(G);" "The Current State of Poetry;" "Overture: Chorus"

Texts available in Jack Foley, *O Powerful Western Star* and Jack Foley, *Eyes* (Selected Poems)

https:// soundcloud.com / john-w-foley/from-o-powerful-western-star-overture-chorus

JACK FOLEY & SANGYE LAND, *DATE: DINNER & A MOVIE 2020*

https://soundcloud.com/john-w-foley/dinner-and-a-movie-mp3?fbclid=IwAR2lW3tNW—VaVlF67baY6MEdnS1NJGLsf17Py6lPMTYdbw7ztf1M_5i9RA

Video

JACK AND ADELLE FOLEY: MARY RUDGE'S STAR ROVER TV (1990)

The program is in 5 parts:

1. https://www.youtube.com/watch?v=E-
   QgiWz8rs8&feature=related
   (Irish speech begins at 2:15)
2. https://www.youtube.com/watch?v=GexgUeDwL8c
3. https://www.youtube.com/watch?v=fzZQj2nXVrk
4. https://www.youtube.com/watch?v=hSqgqPXrQ9Y
5. https://www.youtube.com/watch?v=5GMpMPcxm_w
   (tap dance poem included in this segment: 2:36)

JACK FOLEY DAY / JUNE 5, 2010 CELEBRATION

Event Documents page that documents the public celebration of Jack Foley's life and work on June 5, 2010 with photos, official proclamation, speech, and videos:

http://eventdocuments.blogspot.com

Jack & Adelle performing:
https://www.youtube.com/watch?v=xEpvE2OgQGI&t=340s

JACK & ADELLE FOLEY ANIMATED BY BEAU BLUE
"Ballad of the Beatles"
https://www.youtube.com/watch?v=yo8eC806wmY

There are many other videos available on YouTube and on the internet generally.

A publicity photo of my father. New York, 1926. My father didn't remember who the piano player was.

Jack, Asbury Park, New Jersey. Early 1940s. Perhaps 1940. Photographer unknown, perhaps my mother. I don't know who is holding me.

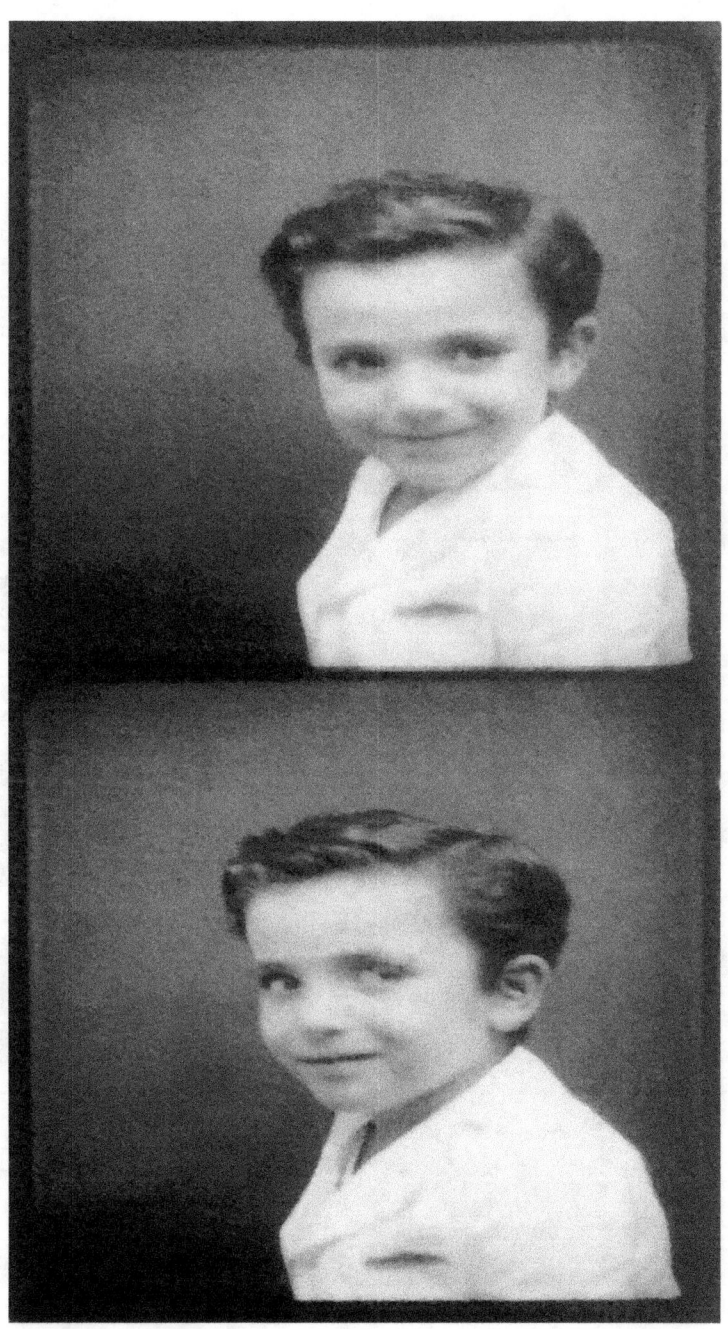

Amusement park photo-booth photo. Playland, Rye Beach. Early to middle 1940s.

My mother and me, ca. 1945. Perhaps in Fords, New Jersey at the home of "Aunt Edna," not a blood relative but a friend of my parents.

Jack, Confirmation photo, ca. 1953, Port Chester, New York. Our Lady of Mercy
Catholic Church is behind Jack. I'm told Ed Sullivan sometimes attended Mass there, but
I never saw him.

Jack in the three-room apartment in Port Chester. Behind me is an ancient Webcor tape recorder. Having been entranced by Noël Coward's first television special, *Together With Music* (1955, with Mary Martin), Jack hunted up Coward's autobiography. Jack also perfected an imitation of Coward's voice which he can still deliver. Photo ca. 1956, probably taken by my mother.

Port Chester High School Yearbook (*Peningian*) photo. 1958

Jack and Adelle, wedding photo. Photographer: Weitzmann. New York City, December, 1961.

Jack & Adelle in costume for the musical he co-wrote, *Tom Jones*. Cornell University, June, 1962. Rerun performance for a weekend to which parents were invited. Photo perhaps by Bryn Matthews, who had directed the production. Jack did his own makeup and, in this costume, performed a tap dance.

Oakland, CA, February 24, 1974. Sean is four days old. Photographer: Fred Betz.

Adelle, Jack and Sean Foley, 1986. This photo was reproduced on the back cover of Jack's first book, *Letters/Lights--Words for Adelle*. Seeing it, someone asked Adelle, "Is that your group?" She answered, "No, that's my family." The t-shirt Adelle is wearing had been purchased from Gamelan Sekar Jaya. One of its members taught at Sean's elementary school--her students, including Sean, wrote a short piece of Balinese-inspired music--and Jack and Adelle had attended many concerts of Balinese music and dance. Jack told Lou Harrison that Sean, like Lou, had written for gamelan. Jack's hat had been purchased because he often brought the disabled Larry Eigner to events. Both Jack's hands were busy steering Larry's wheelchair. If it rained there was no way he could carry an umbrella. The hat was protection against the rain. Photo by Carol Boyd, the wife of Jack's gardener.

Jack, 1987. Photo by Robert Schneck, a friend who realized that Jack was rising in the poetry world and needed an "official" photo.

Jack hosting "The Performance Poetry Bash" event at Herman Berlandt's National Poetry
Week, Fort Mason, San Francisco,1988. Jack coordinated the event, which included
diverse modes of "performance," including poet Anne Waldman, The wordWind Chorus
(Reginald Lockett, q.r. hand, jr., Brian Auerbach, and Lewis Jordan), and the Frank
Moore Troupe, whose painted, nude bodies were a presence throughout.
Photo by Jenny Chu.

From Jack's introduction:

*Performance poetry is an active and intellectually engaged response to the silence and
whiteness in which most poetry remains entangled. Writing of Mallarmé, Frederick R.
Karl remarked, "The page or territory is primary, on which language wanders like a
lonely adventurer hoping to survive emptiness and whiteness." The performance poet
insists that s/he is not a mere adjunct of a book but rather a manifestation of what books
arise out of: the physical presence of the author. Historically, "poetry" and "writing"
remain in a state of tension. (Homer was a poet, not a writer.) Performance poetry seeks
to tilt that tension in the direction of presence, to insist on the limitations of writing as a
medium for the presentation of the art. At the heart of writing, at the heart of all mass
culture, is a profound and disturbing absence. Performance poetry is an insistence that
absence, silence and whiteness—the page—are not the only conditions in which poetry
can be "heard."*

Jack and Adelle performed "Chorus: SON(G)."

Jack and Adelle at Cody's Books, Berkeley, CA. 1988. Photo by Rick Mahan. One of their most successful readings. Adelle on performing with Jack: "I've been performing with Jack for over twenty years. He writes the poems; the collaboration is in the presentation. We have a couple of signature pieces, "standards," like "Overture: Chorus," also known as "hummingbird," and "Chorus: SON(G)." Before we first presented them, we rehearsed a lot and we even recorded them. Jack may read parts of a piece to give me an idea of how he hears it. Then he will assign lines or phrases to each of us and indicate words to be spoken together, as a round or two texts to be performed at the same time. Now, I may make suggestions on aspects of a newer choral piece. I'm also responsible for synchronizing the timing when we are performing different texts. Audiences, particularly musicians, react well to choral pieces. It's a new idea that wakes them up. but the work is noisy, and some people resist the sound. In the last few years, Jack began writing short plays and we've been performing them as well. These allow me to show that I'm something of a ham. When we first started, I was nervous about performing my husband's work, getting it right. But performing the choral pieces and plays is exciting. Sometimes they're challenging, but Jack is really good at presenting poetry orally and I love working with him, the way we sound, and the feedback we get from people."

Jack's drawing of his dear friend, Larry Eigner. Ca. 1992. Jack had brought Larry to Ellen Drori's night class on film at U.C. Berkeley and was sitting behind him.

Jack Foley Day, June 5, 2010, Berkeley, CA. Photo by Eddy Pay. Jack received a Lifetime Achievement Award from The Berkeley Poetry Festival. Various friends performed. The entire festival is available on YouTube. Jack and Adelle gave a special reading which included the following speculations. The concluding passage contains a famous quotation from Baudelaire:

what was the purpose, if purpose there was
why all this fury?
did you hope to change the perceptions
of people at large?
—yes, foolishly.

did you believe that anything you said could affect the immense misconception people call reality? *quelle erreur*!
—yes, it was a mistake.

so what did it *do*? did you teach anyone anything?
—no.

were you able to change the nature of poetry, even in the smallest way?
—no.

so what reveals itself, admirable author, at this difficult point of your being?

—nothing! *j'aime les nuages, les nuages qui passent*. I love the passing / clouds. as for poetry, *ça m'a donné quelque chose à faire*—it gave me something to do!
Jack and Adelle had commemorative t-shirts manufactured for the day. Adelle has a pen on her ear in the photo because she is selling the t-shirts.

February 20, 2017. Sangye Land and Jack at Binh Minh Quan Vietnamese restaurant in Oakland. Sangye and Jack consider their anniversary to be February 14, 2017. Photo by Jack's artist friend, Paul Veres. Paul's sketch of Sangye can dimly be seen in the lower right hand corner of the photo.

Sangye Land and Jack performing. Downtown Oakland, CA. 2019. Photo by poet Maw Shein Win. Jack's writing has changed to some degree in order to accommodate Sangye's beautiful voice and talents as a performer. He does not regard this change as in any way making his writing less "authentic." "World"--which now includes Sangye--is an aspect of all of Jack's writing.

Thanksgiving, 2019. Nashville, Tennessee. American families. Sean and his wife, Kerry, at far right. Photo by Kerry Foley. Thanks to Sean and Kerry's Malaysian friends, the food included wonderful Malay dishes as well as Kerry's excellent traditional Thanksgiving fare--including some dishes Adelle always made at Thanksgiving.

Delicious Malay food mingling with Western
Turkey, good fellowship, good
Conversation, children abounding.
One, named "Wisdom" (Sofea), curtsied to me,
I bowed, she bowed back & passed.
Later, before leaving, she hugged me,
Took my hand, kissed it, put it to her forehead—
Brushed by wings of childhood!
Kindness—in the root sense
As well as in the modern—
Abounded.
All listened as I talked poetry
And as my son spoke lore of all sorts,
Told us of his new book and plans for another,
Sangye at my side, comforting, as I spoke of my late wife
And of her struggle with death (may she rest!)
I am old—near eighty—and have experienced
Many Thanksgivings, none richer
Than these in Nashville,
My son and daughter in law and I united in loss,
United as well in our pull towards life,
My new love comforting, sweet, NEW.
Tears and laughter,
A child named Wisdom who bowed to me.

Selfie, October 1, 2020. Jack in Harvest Moon Light, shining brilliantly that night.

the man looks out
in the difficult moonlight
in the darkness
of a complex historical
moment
the huge moon
delivering nothing but
enigma
the shadows and lights
uncertain in their meaning
he may be frightened
or perhaps weary
(he is old!)
he looks at us
so much of his life
in his face
what else matters?
the dark tree
the moon tonight
the color of blood
and the puzzle
of a man alone
with whatever thoughts
this moonlight brings